The
Modern
Century

The Modern Century

The Whidden Lectures 1967

Northrop Frye

**NEW EDITION
Including The Cultural
Development of Canada
1990**

Toronto
Oxford University Press

Oxford University Press, 70 Wynford Drive,
Don Mills, Ontario M3C 1J9

Toronto   Oxford   New York
Delhi   Bombay   Calcutta   Madras   Karachi   Petaling Jaya
Singapore   Hong Kong   Tokyo   Nairobi   Dar es Salaam
Cape Town   Melbourne   Auckland

and associated companies in
Berlin   Ibadan

Canadian Cataloguing in Publication Data

Frye, Northrop, 1912-1991
  The modern century

Includes The cultural development of Canada, given
at the University of Toronto, Oct. 17, 1990.
ISBN 0-19-540873-X

1. Civilization, Modern – 20th century.   I. Title.

CB425.F78 1991   909.8'2   C91-095273-6

Contents

Foreword

THE WHIDDEN LECTURES were established in 1954 by E. C. Fox, B.A., LL.D., of Toronto, the senior member of the Board of Governors, to honour the memory of a former Chancellor of McMaster University.

The Reverend Dr Howard P. Whidden, D.D., LL.D., D.C.L., F.R.S.C., was a man of striking appearance, unusual dignity, deep Christian conviction, and ready tolerance. Born in 1871 in Antigonish, Nova Scotia, where his family had settled in 1761 after three-quarters of a century's residence in New England, he attended

universities in both Canada (Acadia and McMaster) and
the United States (Chicago), and also served as a min-
ister of Baptist churches in both countries (in Ontario,
Manitoba, and Ohio). From 1913 to 1923 he was Presi-
dent of Brandon College, Manitoba, then an affiliate of
McMaster University, and for part of that period (1917-
21) he represented Brandon as a member of Parliament
in the Canadian House of Commons at Ottawa. He was
appointed administrative head (Chancellor) of Mc-
Master University in 1923 and in 1930 became, in a
manner of speaking, its second founder when he directed its transfer from Toronto, where it had been
established since 1887, to Hamilton. His broad educational outlook and effective leadership resulted in the
University's burgeoning greatly in its new location, and
Dr Whidden was able to retire in 1941 with the comforting conviction that he had built both wisely and
well. He died in Toronto in 1952.

The selection of a Canadian scholar to be the Whidden Lecturer in 1967, the year of Canada's centennial,
was inevitable. And that the choice should fall on
H. Northrop Frye, the first person ever to be named by
the University of Toronto as its University Professor,
was almost equally inevitable. His reputation as one of
the most significant of contemporary literary critics is
world-wide and securely established. It is a cause for
pride to academic circles in his native country that he
should be the subject of a special volume, issued by the
Columbia University Press just over a year ago. A gradu-
ate of Toronto and Merton College, Oxford, he made

his mark some twenty years ago with a penetrating study of William Blake, *Fearful Symmetry*; and since that time a steady stream of books and articles from his pen has made his name one of the most familiar and most respected wherever the study of English letters is seriously pursued. He has lectured in scores of universities throughout the English-speaking world and has received honorary doctorates from many of them.

For the 1967 Whidden Lectures he chose as his theme *The Modern Century*, the century in which, as the saying goes, Canada came of age. He did not restrict his vision, however, to the literary and creative activities that have occurred in this country over the past one hundred years. Rather, he attempted to relate Canadian developments to those of the world as a whole; and it was a stimulating and exciting exercise to accompany him as his purview ranged over other countries, other continents, and other cultures. That the perspective of the many hundreds who had the privilege of hearing him was deepened and broadened, there is not the slightest doubt.

McMaster University is now very pleased to publish the lectures in book form so that an even wider audience may share in the rewarding experience of learning the views of a distinguished Canadian on man's spiritual and intellectual adventures since 1867.

February 1967

E. T. SALMON
Principal of University College
McMaster University

Author's Note

THE OPERATION of giving the Whidden Lectures for 1967 was made pleasant and memorable by the hospitality of McMaster University and my many friends there. To them, as well as to the extraordinarily attentive and responsive audience, I feel deeply grateful.

I am indebted to the Canada Council for a grant which enabled me to work on this and other projects, and to Mrs Jessie Jackson for her preparation of the manuscript.

The lectures were delivered in the centenary year of

Canada's Confederation, and were originally intended to be Canadian in subject-matter. I felt, however, that I had really said all I had to say about Canadian culture for some time, with the help of about forty colleagues, in the 'Conclusion' to the recently published *Literary History of Canada: Canadian Literature in English* (1965). Hence the shift of theme to a wider context. I have tried to make my Canadian references as explicit as possible, for the benefit of non-Canadian readers, but have not invariably succeeded. For example, the titles of the three lectures are titles of poems by well-known Canadian poets: respectively, Archibald Lampman, Irving Layton, and Émile Nelligan.

N. F.

Victoria College in the
University of Toronto
January 1967

1

City
of the
end
of things

THE WHIDDEN LECTURES have been a distinguished series, and anyone attempting to continue them must feel a sense of responsibility. For me, the responsibility is specific: I have been asked to keep in mind the fact that I shall be speaking to a Canadian audience in the Centennial year of Confederation. I have kept it in mind, and the first thing that it produced there was what I hope is a sense of proportion. The centenary of Confederation is a private celebration, a family party, in what is still a relatively small country in a very big world. One most reassuring quality in

Canadians, and the one which, I find, chiefly makes them liked and respected abroad, when they are, is a certain unpretentiousness, a cheerful willingness to concede the immense importance of the non-Canadian part of the human race. It is appropriate to a Canadian audience, then, to put our centenary into some kind of perspective. For the majority of people in North America, the most important thing that happened in 1867 was the purchase of Alaska from Russia by the United States. For the majority of people in the orbit of British traditions, the most important thing that happened in 1867 was the passing of the Second Reform Bill, the measure that Disraeli called 'a leap in the dark', but which was really the first major effort to make the Mother of Parliaments represent the people instead of an oligarchy. For a great number, very probably the majority, of people in the world today, the most important thing that happened in 1867, anywhere, was the publication of the first volume of *Das Kapital* by Karl Marx, the only part of the book actually published by Marx himself. It was this event, of course, that helped among other things to make the purchase of Alaska so significant: another example of the principle that life imitates literature, in the broad sense, and not the other way round. There is a still bigger majority to be considered, the majority of the dead. In the year 1867 Thomas Hardy wrote a poem called '1967', in which he remarks that the best thing he can say about that year is the fact that he is not going to live to see it.

My own primary interests are in literary and educational culture. What I should like to discuss with you here is not Canadian culture in itself, but the context of that culture in the world of the last century. One reason for my wanting to talk about the world that Canada is in rather than about Canada is that I should like to bypass some common assumptions about Canadian culture which we are bound to hear repeated a good deal in the course of this year. There is, for instance, the assumption that Canada has, in its progress from colony to nation, grown and matured like an individual: that to be colonial means to be immature, and to be national means to be grown up. A colony or a province, we are told, produced a naïve, imitative, and prudish culture; now we have become a nation, we should start producing sophisticated, original, and spontaneous culture. (I dislike using 'sophisticated' in an approving sense, but it does seem to be an accepted term for a kind of knowledgeability that responds to culture with the minimum of anxieties.) If we fail to produce a fully mature culture, the argument usually runs, it must be because we are still colonial or provincial in our attitude, and the best thing our critics and creators can do is to keep reminding us of this. If a Canadian painter or poet gets some recognition, he is soon giving interviews asserting that Canadian society is hypocritical, culturally constipated, and sexually inhibited. This might be thought a mere cliché, indicating that originality is a highly specialized gift, but it seems to have advanced in Canada to the place of an obligatory ritual. Some time ago, when a Canadian play opened in Paris, a reviewer, himself a Canadian, remarked sardonically: 'Comme c'est canadien! Comme c'est pur!' I should add that this comment was incorporated by the Canadian publisher as a part of his blurb.

Analogies between the actual growth of an individual and the supposed growth of a society may be illuminating, but they must always be, like all analogies, open to fresh examination. The analogy is a particularly tricky form of rhetoric when it becomes the basis of an argument rather than merely a figure of speech. Certainly every society produces a type of culture which is roughly characteristic of itself. A provincial society has a provincial culture; a metropolitan society has a metropolitan culture. A provincial society will produce a phenomenon like the tea party described in F. R. Scott's well-known satire, 'The Canadian Authors Meet'. A metropolitan society would turn the tea party into a cocktail party, and the conversation would be louder, faster, more knowing, and cleverer at rationalizing its pretentiousness and egotism. But its poets would not necessarily be of any more lasting value than Mr Scott's Miss Crotchet, though they might be less naïve. It is true that relatively few if any of the world's greatest geniuses have been born in Canada, although a remarkable British painter and writer, Wyndham Lewis, went so far as to get himself born on a ship off Canadian shores, and developed an appropriately sea-sick view of Canada in later life. But we do not know enough about what social conditions produce great or even good writers to connect a lack of celebrated birthplaces with the moral quality of Canadian civilization.

Another aspect of the same assumption is more subtle and pervasive. It is widely believed, or assumed, that Canada's destiny, culturally and historically, finds its fulfilment in being a nation, and that nationality is essential to identity. It seems to me, on the other hand, quite clear that we are moving towards a post-national world, and that Canada has moved further in that direction than most of the smaller nations. What is important about the last century, in this country, is not that we have been a nation for a hundred years, but that we have had a hundred years in which to make the transition from a pre-national to a post-national consciousness. The so-called emergent nations, such countries as Nigeria or Indonesia, have not been so fortunate: for them, the tensions of federalism and separatism, of middle-class and working-class interests, of xenophobia and adjustment to the larger world, have all come in one great rush. Canada has—so far—been able to avoid both this kind of chaos and the violence that goes with the development of a vast imperial complex like the U.S.A. or the U.S.S.R. The Canadian sense of proportion that I mentioned is especially valuable now, as helping us to adopt an attitude consistent with the world it is actually in. My present task, I think, is neither to eulogize nor to elegize Canadian nationality, neither to celebrate its survival nor to lament its passage, but to consider what kinds of social context are appropriate for a world in which the nation is rapidly ceasing to be the real defining unit of society.

We begin, then, with the conception of a 'modern' world, which began to take shape a century ago and now provides the context for Canadian existence, and consequently for our Centennial. A century ago Canada was a nation in the world, but not wholly of it: the major cultural and political developments of Western Europe, still the main centre of the historical stage, were little known or understood in Canada, and the Canadian reaction even to such closer events as the American Civil War was largely negative. Today, Canada is too much a part of the world to be thought of as a nation in it. We have our undefended border with the United States, so celebrated in Canadian oratory, only because it is not a real boundary line at all: the real boundary line, one of the most heavily defended in the world, runs through the north of the country, separating a bourgeois sphere of control from a Marxist one.

Culturally, the primary fact about the modern world, or at least about our 'Western' and 'democratic' part of it, is that it is probably the first civilization in history that has attempted to study itself objectively, to become aware of the presuppositions underlying its behaviour, to understand its relation to previous history and to see whether its future could in some measure be controlled by its own will. This self-consciousness has created a sharp cultural dialectic in society, an intellectual antagonism between two mental attitudes. On one side are those who struggle for an active and conscious relation to their time, who study what is happening in the world, survey the conditions of life that seem most likely to occur, and try to acquire some sense of what can be done to build up from those conditions a way of life that is at least self-respecting. On the other side are those who adopt a passive and negative attitude, responding to the daily news and similar stimuli, aware of what is going on but making no effort to understand either the underlying causes or the future possibilities. The theatre of this conflict in attitudes is formed by the creative and the communicating arts. The creative arts are almost entirely on the active side: they mean nothing, or infinitely less, to a passive response. The subject-matter of contemporary literature being its own time, the passive and uncritical attitude is seen as its most dangerous enemy. Many aspects of contemporary literature—its ironic tone, its emphasis on anxiety and absurdity, its queasy apocalyptic forebodings—derive from this situation.

The communicating arts, including the so-called mass media, are a mixture of things. Some of them are arts in their own right, like the film. Some are or include different techniques of presenting the arts we already have, like television. Some are not arts, but present analogies to techniques in the arts which the arts may enrich themselves by employing, as the newspaper may influence collage in painting or the field theory of composition in poetry. Some are applied arts, where the appeal is no longer disinterested, as it normally is in the creative arts proper. Thus propaganda is an interested use of the literary techniques of rhetoric. As usual, there are deficiencies in vocabulary: there are no words that really convey the intellectual and moral contrast of the active and passive attitudes to culture. The phrase 'mass culture' conveys emotional overtones of passivity: it suggests someone eating peanuts at a baseball game, and thereby contrasting himself to someone eating canapés at the opening of a sculpture exhibition. The trouble with this picture is that the former is probably part of a better educated audience, in the sense that he is likely to know more about baseball than his counterpart knows about sculpture. Hence his attitude to his chosen area of culture may well be the more active of the two. And just as there can be an active response to mass culture, so there can be passive responses to the highbrow arts. These range from 'Why can't the artist make his work mean something to the ordinary man?' to the significant syntax of the student's question: 'Why is this considered a good poem?' The words advertising and propaganda come closest to suggesting a communication deliberately imposed and passively received. They represent respectively the communicating interests of the two major areas of society, the economic and the political. Recently these two conceptions have begun to merge into the single category of 'public relations'.

One very obvious feature of our age is the speeding up of process: it is an age of revolution and metamorphosis, where one lives through changes that formerly took centuries in a matter of a few years. In a world where dynasties rise and fall at much the same rate as women's hemlines, the dynasty and the hemline look much alike in importance, and get much the same amount of featuring in the news. Thus the progression of events is two-dimensional, a child's drawing reflecting an eye that observes without seeing depth, and even the effort to see depth has still to deal with the whole surface. Some new groupings result: for example, what used to be called the trivial or ephemeral takes on a function of *symbolizing* the significant. A new art of divination or augury has developed, in which the underlying trends of the contemporary world are interpreted by vogues and fashions in dress, speech or entertainment. Thus if there appears a vogue for white lipstick among certain groups of young women, that may represent a new impersonality in sexual relationship, a parody of white supremacy, the dramatization of a death-wish, or the social projection of the clown archetype. Any number may play, but the game is a somewhat self-defeating one, without much power of sustaining its own interest. For even the effort to identify something in the passing show has the effect of dating it, as whatever is sufficiently formed to be recognized has already receded into the past.

It is not surprising if some people should be frustrated by the effort to keep riding up and down the manic-depressive roller-coaster of fashion, of what's in and what's out, what is u and what non-u, what is hip and what is square, what is corny and what is camp. There are perhaps not as many of these unhappy people as our newspapers and magazines suggest there are: in any case, what is important is not this group, if it exists, but the general sense, in our society, of the panic of change. The variety of things that occur in the world, combined with the relentless continuity of their appearance day after day, impress us with the sense of a process going by a little too fast for our minds to focus on anything in it.

Some time ago, the department of English in a Canadian university decided to offer a course in twentieth-century poetry. It was discovered that there were two attitudes in the department towards that subject: there were those who felt that twentieth-century poetry had begun with Eliot's *The Waste Land* in 1922, and those who felt that most of the best of it had already been written by that time. There also appeared to be some correlation between these two views and the age groups of those who held them. Finally a compromise was reached: two courses were offered, one called Modern Poetry and the other Contemporary Poetry. But even the contemporary course would need now to be supplemented by a third course in the post-contemporary, and perhaps a fourth in current happenings. In the pictorial arts the fashion-parade of isms is much faster: I hear of painters, even in Canada, who have frantically changed their styles completely three or four times in a few years, as collectors demanded first abstract expressionism, then pop art, then pornography, then hard-edge, selling off their previous purchases as soon as the new vogue took hold. There is a medieval legend of the Wild Hunt, in which souls of the dead had to keep marching to nowhere all day and all night at top speed. Anyone who dropped out of line from exhaustion instantly crumbled to dust. This seems a parable of a type of consciousness frequent in the modern world, obsessed by a compulsion to keep up, reduced to despair by the steadily increasing speed of the total movement. It is a type of consciousness which I shall call the alienation of progress.

Alienation and progress are two central elements in the mythology of our day, and both words have been extensively used and misused. The conception of alienation was originally a religious one, and perhaps that is still the context in which it makes most sense. In religion, the person aware of sin feels alienated, not necessarily from society, but from the presence of God, and it is in this feeling of alienation that the religious life begins. The conception is clearest in evangelical thinkers in the Lutheran tradition like Bunyan, who see alienation of this kind as the beginning of a psychological revolution. Once one becomes aware of being in sin and under the wrath of God, one realizes that one's master is the devil, the prince of this world, and that treason and rebellion against this master is the first requirement of the new life.

A secularized use of the idea appears in the early work of Marx, where alienation describes the feeling of the worker who is cheated out of most of the fruit of his labour by exploitation. He is unable to participate in society to the extent that, as a worker, he should, because his status in society has been artificially degraded. In this context the alienated are those who have been dispossessed by their masters, and who therefore recognize their masters as their enemies, as Christian did Apollyon. In our day those who are alienated in Marx's sense are, for example, the Negro, whose status is also arbitrarily degraded, or those who are in actual want and misery. The Negro, looking at the selfishness and panic in white eyes, realizes that while what he has to fight is ultimately a state of mind, still his enemies also include people who have got themselves identified with this state of mind. Thus his enemies, again, are those who believe themselves his masters or natural superiors. Apart from such special situations, not many in the Western democracies today believe that a specific social act, such as expropriating a propertied class, would end alienation in the modern world.

The reason is that in a society like ours, a society of the accepted and adequately fed, the conception of alienation becomes psychological. In other words it becomes the devil again, for the devil normally comes to those who have everything and are bored with it, like Faust. The root of this aspect of alienation is the sense that man has lost control, if he ever had it, over his own destiny. The master or tyrant is still an enemy, but not an enemy that anyone can fight. Theoretically, the world is divided into democracies and peoples' republics: actually, there has never been a time when man felt less sense of participation in the really fateful decisions that affect his life and his death. The central symbol of this is of course the overkill bomb, as presented in such works as *Dr Strangelove*, the fact that the survival of humanity itself may depend on a freak accident. In a world where the tyrant-enemy can be recognized, even defined, and yet cannot be projected on anything or anybody, he remains part of ourselves, or more precisely of our own death-wish, a cancer that gradually disintegrates the sense of community. We may try to persuade ourselves that the complete destruction of Communism (or, on their side, of capitalist imperialism) would also destroy alienation. But an instant of genuine reflection would soon tell us that all such external enemies could disappear from the earth tomorrow and leave us exactly where we were before.

In this situation there is a steady pressure in the direction of making one's habitual responses passive. The first to succumb to this pressure are those whose attitude to the world is deliberately frivolous, who have only an instinct for avoiding any kind of stimulus that might provoke a genuine concern. Such an attitude tries to ignore the issues of the day and responds mainly to the 'human interest' stories in the tabloids provided for it, gathering its experience of life much as one might pick up a number of oddly shaped stones on a beach. But even here the effort to shut out anxiety is itself an anxiety, and a very intense one, which keeps the conscious and critical part of the mind very near to the breaking point of hysteria. The mind on the verge of breakdown is infinitely suggestible, as Pavlov demonstrated, and the forces of advertising and propaganda move in without any real opposition from the critical intelligence.

These agencies act in much the same way that, in *Paradise Lost*, Milton depicts Satan acting on Eve. All that poor Eve was consciously aware of was the fact that a hitherto silent snake was talking to her. Her consciousness being fascinated by something outrageous, everything that Satan had to suggest got through its guard and fell into what we should call her subconscious. Later, when faced with a necessity of making a free choice, she found nothing inside her to direct the choice except Satan's arguments, which she perforce had to take as her own, the more readily in that she did not realize how they had got there. Similarly, the technique of advertising and propaganda is to stun and demoralize the critical consciousness with statements too absurd or extreme to be dealt with seriously by it. In the mind that is too frightened or credulous or childish to want to deal with the world at all, they move in past the consciousness and set up their structures unopposed.

What they create in such a mind is not necessarily acceptance, but dependence on their versions of reality. Advertising implies an economy which has some independence from the political structure, and as long as this independence exists, advertising can be taken as a kind of ironic game. Like other forms of irony, it says what it does not wholly mean, but nobody is obliged to believe its statements literally. Hence it creates an illusion of detachment and mental superiority even when one is obeying its exhortations. When doing Christmas shopping, there is hardly one of us who would not, if stopped by an interviewer, say that of course he didn't hold with all this commercializing of Christmas. The same is to some extent true of propaganda as long as the issues are not deeply serious. The curiously divided reaction to the Centennial—a mixture of the sentimental, the apprehensive, and the sardonic—is an example. But in more serious matters, such as the Vietnam war, the effects of passivity are more subtly demoralizing. The tendency is to accept the propaganda bromide rather than the human truths involved, not merely because it is more comfortable, but because it gives the illusion of taking a practical and activist attitude as opposed to mere hand-wringing. When propaganda cuts off all other sources of information, rejecting it, for a concerned and responsible citizen, would not only isolate him from his social world, but isolate him so completely as to destroy his self-respect. Hence even propaganda based on the big lie, as when an American or Chinese politician tries to get rid of a rival by calling him a Communist or a bourgeois counter-revolutionary, can establish itself and command assent if it makes more noise than the denial of the charge. The epigram that it is impossible to fool all the people all the time may be consoling, but is not much more.

What eventually happens I may describe in a figure borrowed from those interminable railway journeys that are so familiar to Canadians, at least of my generation. As one's eyes are passively pulled along a rapidly moving landscape, it turns darker and one begins to realize that many of the objects that appear to be out-side are actually reflections of what is in the carriage. As it becomes entirely dark one enters a narcissistic world, where, except for a few lights here and there, we can see only the reflection of where we are. A little study of the working of advertising and propaganda in the modern world, with their magic-lantern techniques of projected images, will show us how successful they are in creating a world of pure illusion. The illusion of the world itself is reinforced by the more explicit illusions of movies and television, and the imitation world of sports. It is significant that a breakdown in illusion, as when a baseball game or a television program is proved to have been 'fixed', is more emotionally disturbing than proof of crime or corruption in the actual world. It is true that not all illusion is a bad thing: elections, for example, would hardly arouse enough interest to keep a democracy functioning unless they were assimilated to sporting events, and unless the pseudo-issues were taken as real issues. Similarly the advantages of winning the game of space ships and moon landings may be illusory, but the illusion is better than spending the money involved on preparations for war. Then again, when illusion has been skilfully built up, as it is for instance by such agencies as the *Reader's Digest*, it includes the illusion of keeping abreast of contemporary thought and events, and can only be recognized as illusion by its effects, or rather by the absence of any effects, in social action.

Democracy is a mixture of majority rule and minority right, and the minority which most clearly has a right is the minority of those who try to resist a passive response, and thereby risk the resentment of those who regard them as trying to be undemocratically superior. I am speaking however not so much of two groups of people as of two mental attitudes, both of which may exist in the same mind. The prison of illusion holds all of us: the first important step is to be aware of it as illusion, and as a prison. The right of free criticism is immensely important, and the habitually worried and anxious attitude of the more responsible citizen has a significance out of proportion to its frequency. But the alienation of progress operates on him too, in a different way. He finds, in the first place, his response of concern becoming a stock response. Many of us have had the experience of beginning to read a journal of critical comment, tuning ourselves in to the appropriate state of anxiety, and then noticing that we have in error picked up an issue of several months back. In the split second of adjustment we become aware of a conventionalized or voluntarily assumed response. I am not deprecating the response: I am trying to describe a cultural condition. But any conventionalized or habitual response is subject in the course of time to the pressure of becoming automatic. As I write this, an official communiqué about education arrives in the mail, and I read: 'If we are to keep pace with the swiftly moving developments of our time, we must strive for ever higher standards in every field of endeavour. . . . No informed person is unaware of the tremendous effort that [it] will take to meet the demands that the years ahead will produce. Yet we are also aware that the general well-being of our nation is dependent on our ability to meet the challenge.'

One would say that it was impossible to write flatter clichés or more obvious platitudes, and the effect of cliché and platitude ought to be soothing. So it is, and yet every word is soaked in the metaphors of a gasping panic, as though the author had placed a large bet on a contender in a race who was, like Hamlet, fat and scant of breath. The conscious appeal is to the concerned and intelligent citizen, who ought to take an interest in what his public servants are trying to do. A less conscious motive is to prepare him for an increase in taxes. But the combination of urgency in the rhetoric and of dullness in the expression of it is, or would be if we were not so familiar with it, very strange. Something has happened to atrophy one's responses when the most soporific words one can use are such words as 'challenge', 'crisis', 'demand', and 'endeavour'. Even the most genuinely concerned and critical mind finds itself becoming drowsy in its darkening carriage. And not only so, but the very ability to recognize the cliché works against one's sense of full participation. Self-awareness thus operates like a drug, stimulating one's sense of responsibility while weakening the will to express it.

The conception of progress grew up in the nineteenth century around a number of images and ideas. The basis of the conception is the fact that science, in contrast to the arts, develops and advances, with the work of each generation adding to that of its predecessor. Science bears the practical fruit of technology, and technology has created, in the modern world, a new consciousness of time. Man has doubtless always experienced time in the same way, dragged backwards from a receding past into an unknown future. But the quickening of the pace of news, with telegraph and submarine cable, helped to dramatize a sense of a world in visible motion, with every day bringing new scenes and episodes of a passing show. It was as though the ticking of a clock had become not merely audible but obsessive, like the telltale heart in Poe. The first reactions to the new sensation—for it was more of a sensation than a conception —were exhilarating, as all swift movement is for a time. The prestige of the myth of progress developed a number of value-assumptions: the dynamic is better than the static, process better than product, the organic and vital better than the mechanical and fixed, and so on. We still have these value-assumptions, and no doubt they are useful, though like other assumptions we should be aware that we have them. And yet there was an underlying tendency to alienation in the conception of progress itself. In swift movement we are dependent on a vehicle and not on ourselves, and the proportion of exhilaration to apprehensiveness depends on whether we are driving it or merely riding in it. All progressive machines turn out to be things ridden in, with an unknown driver.

Whatever is progressive develops a certain autonomy,

and the reactions to it consequently divide: some feel that it will bring about vast improvements in life by itself, others are more concerned with the loss of human control over it. An example of such a progressive machine was the self-regulating market of laissez faire. The late Karl Polanyi has described, in *The Great Transformation*, how this market dominated the political and economic structure of Western Europe, breaking down the sense of national identity and replacing it with a uniform contractual relationship of management and labour. The autonomous market took out a ninety-nine year lease on the world from 1815 to 1914, and kept 'peace' for the whole of that time. By peace I mean the kind of peace that we have had ourselves since 1945: practically continuous warfare somewhere or other, but with no single war becoming large enough to destroy the overall economic structure, or the major political structures dependent on it. And yet what the autonomous market created in modern consciousness was, even when optimistic, the feeling that Polanyi has finely described as 'an uncritical reliance on the alleged self-healing virtues of unconscious growth'. That is, the belief in social progress was transferred from the human will to the autonomous social force. Similar conceptions of autonomous mass movement and historical process dominate much of our social thinking today. In Communist theology the historical process occupies much the same position that the Holy Spirit does in Christianity: an omnipotent power that co-operates with the human will but is not dependent on it.

Even earlier than the rise of the market, the feeling that man could achieve a better society than the one he was in by a sufficiently resolute act had done much to inspire the American and more particularly the French revolutions, as well as a number of optimistic progressive visions of history like that of Condorcet. Here the ideal society is associated with a not too remote future. Here too there are underlying paradoxes. If we ask what we are progressing to, the only conceivable goal is greater stability, something more orderly and predictable than what we have now. After all, the only thing we can imagine which is better than what we have now is an ensured and constant supply of the best that we do have: economic security, peace, equal status in the protection of law, the appeal of the will to reason, and the like. Progress thus assumes that the dynamic is better than the stable and unchanging, yet it moves toward a greater stability. One famous progressive thinker, John Stuart Mill, had a nervous breakdown when he realized that he did not want to see his goals achieved, but merely wished to act as though he did. What was progress yesterday may seem today like heading straight for a prison of arrested development, like the societies of insects. In the year 1888 Edward Bellamy published *Looking Backward*, a vision of a collectivized future which profoundly inspired the progressive thinkers of that day, and had a social effect such as few works of literature have ever had. Today it impresses us in exactly the opposite way, as a most sinister blueprint for a totalitarian state.

33

A more serious consequence is that under a theory of progress present means have constantly to be sacrificed to future ends, and we do not know the future well enough to know whether those ends will be achieved or not. All we actually know is that we are damaging the present. Thus the assumption that progress is necessarily headed in a good or benevolent direction becomes more and more clearly an unjustified assumption. As early as Malthus the conception of sinister progress had made its appearance, the vision of a world moving onward to a goal of too many people without enough to eat. When it is proposed to deface a city by, say, turning park lots into parking lots, the rationalization given is usually the cliché 'you can't stop progress'. Here it is not even pretended that progress is anything beneficent: it is simply a Juggernaut, or symbol of alienation. And in history the continued sacrificing of a visible present to an invisible future becomes with increasing clarity a kind of Moloch-worship. Some of the most horrible notions that have ever entered the human mind have been 'progressive' notions: massacring farmers to get a more efficient agricultural system, exterminating Jews to achieve a 'solution' of the 'Jewish question', letting a calculated number of people starve to regulate food prices. The element of continuity in progress suggests that the only practicable action is continuous with what we are already doing: if, for instance, we are engaged in a war, it is practicable to go on with the war, and only visionary to stop it.

Hence for most thoughtful people progress has lost

most of its original sense of a favourable value-judge-ment and has become simply progression, towards a goal more likely to be a disaster than an improvement. Taking thought for the morrow, we are told on good authority, is a dangerous practice. In proportion as the confidence in progress has declined, its relation to indi-vidual experience has become clearer. That is, progress is a social projection of the individual's sense of the pass-ing of time. But the individual, as such, is not progress-ing to anything except his own death. Hence the col-lapse of belief in progress reinforces the sense of anxiety which is rooted in the consciousness of death. Alien-ation and anxiety become the same thing, caused by a new intensity in the awareness of the movement of time, as it ticks our lives away day after day. This in-tensifying of the sense of time also, as we have just seen, dislocates it: the centre of attention becomes the future, and the emotional relation to the future becomes one of dread and uncertainty. The future is the point at which 'it is later than you think' becomes 'too late'. Modern fiction has constantly dealt, during the last century, with characters struggling toward some act of con-sciousness or self-awareness that would be a gateway to real life. But the great majority of treatments of this theme are ironic: the act is not made, or is made too late, or is a paralyzing awareness with no result except self-contempt, or is perverted into illusion. We notice that when the tone is less ironic and more hopeful about the nature and capacities of man, as it is for instance in Camus's *La Peste*, it is usually in a context of physical emergency where there is a definite enemy to fight.

Even in theory progress is as likely to lead to the uniform and the monotonous as to the individual and varied. If we look at the civilization around us, the evidence for uniformity is as obvious and oppressive as the evidence for the rapid change toward it. The basis of this uniformity is technological, but the rooted social institutions of the past—home, school, church—can also only be adapted to a nomadic society by an expanding uniform pattern. Whatever the advantages of this situation, we have also to consider the consequences of the world's becoming increasingly what in geology is called a peneplain, a monotonous surface worn down to a dead level by continued erosion. We are not far into the nineteenth century before we become aware of a different element both in consciousness and in the physical appearance of society. This is a new geometrical perspective, already beginning in the eighteenth century, which is scaled, not to the human body, but increasingly to the mechanical extensions of the body. It is particularly in America, of course, that this perspective is most noticeable: Washington, laid out by L'Enfant in 1800, is already in the age of the automobile. This mechanical perspective is mainly the result of the spreading of the city and its technology over more and more of its natural environment. The railway is the earliest and still one of the most dramatic examples of the creation of a new kind of landscape, one which imposes geometrical shapes on the countryside. The prophet Isaiah sees the coming of the Messiah as symbolized by a highway which exalts valleys and depresses mountains, making the crooked straight and the rough places plain. But, as so often happens, the prophecy appears to have been fulfilled in the wrong context.

The traditional city is centripetal, focused on market squares, a pattern still visible in some Ontario towns. Its primary idea is that of community, and it is this idea that has made so many visions of human fulfilment, from Plato and the Bible onward, take the form of a city. To the modern imagination the city becomes increasingly something hideous and nightmarish, the *fourmillante cité* of Baudelaire, the 'unreal city' of Eliot's *Waste Land*, the *ville tentaculaire* of Verhaeren. No longer a community, it seems more like a community turned inside out, with its expressways taking its thousands of self-enclosed nomadic units in a headlong flight into greater solitude, ants in the body of a dying dragon, breathing its polluted air and passing its polluted water. The map still shows us self-contained cities like Hamilton and Toronto, but experience presents us with an urban sprawl which ignores national boundaries and buries a vast area of beautiful and fertile land in a tomb of concrete. I have had occasion to read Dickens a good deal lately, and Dickens was, I suppose, the first metropolitan novelist in English literature, the first to see the life of his time as essentially a gigantic pulsation toward and away from the great industrial centres, specifically London. And one notices in his later novels an increasing sense of the metropolis as a kind of cancer, as something that not only destroys the countryside, but the city itself as it had developed up to that time.

The Victorian critics of the new industrialism contemporary with Dickens, such as Ruskin and Morris, concentrated much of their attack on its physical ugliness, which they saw as a symbol of the spiritual ugliness of materialism and exploitation. Critics of our time are more impressed by the physical uniformity which they similarly interpret as a symbol of spiritual conformity. If certain tendencies within our civilization were to proceed unchecked, they would rapidly take us towards a society which, like that of a prison, would be both completely introverted and completely without privacy. The last stand of privacy has always been, traditionally, the inner mind. It is quite possible however for communications media, especially the newer electronic ones, to break down the associative structures of the inner mind and replace them by the prefabricated structures of the media. A society entirely controlled by their slogans and exhortations would be introverted, because nobody would be saying anything: there would only be echo, and Echo was the mistress of Narcissus. It would also be without privacy, because it would frustrate the effort of the healthy mind to develop a view of the world which is private but not introverted, accommodating itself to opposing views. The triumph of communication is the death of communication: where communication forms a total environment, there is nothing to be communicated.

The role of communications media in the modern world is a subject that Professor Marshall McLuhan has made so much his own that it would be almost a discourtesy not to refer to him in a lecture which covers many of his themes. The McLuhan cult, or more accurately the McLuhan rumour, is the latest of the illusions of progress: it tells us that a number of new media are about to bring in a new form of civilization all by themselves, merely by existing. Because of this we should not, in staring at a television set, wonder if we are wasting our time and develop guilt feelings accordingly: we should feel that we are evolving a new mode of apprehension. What is important about the television set is not the quality of what it exudes, which is only content, but the fact that it is there, the end of a tube with a vortical suction which 'involves' the viewer. This is not all of what a serious and most original writer is trying to say, yet Professor McLuhan lends himself partly to this interpretation by throwing so many of his insights into a deterministic form. He would connect the alienation of progress with the habit of forcing a hypnotized eye to travel over thousands of miles of type, in what is so accurately called the pursuit of knowledge. But apparently he would see the Gutenberg syndrome as a cause of the alienation of progress, and not simply as one of its effects. Determinism of this kind, like the determinism which derives Confederation from the railway, is a plausible but over-simplified form of rhetoric.

Similarly with the principle of the identity of medium and message, which means one thing when the response is active, and quite another when the response is passive. On the active level it is an ideal formulation which strictly applies only to the arts, and to a fully active response to the arts. It would be true to say that painting, for example, had no 'message' except the medium of painting itself. On the passive level it is an ironic formulation in which the differences among the media flatten out. The 'coolness' of television is much more obvious in the privacy of a middle-class home than it is when turned on full blast in the next room of a jerry-built hotel. All forms of communication, from transistors to atom bombs, are equally hot when someone else's finger is on the button. Thus the primary determining quality of the medium comes from the social motive for using it and not from the medium itself. Media can only follow the direction of the human will that created them, and a study of the social direction of that will, or what Innis called the bias of communication, is a major, prior, and separate problem.

Technology cannot of itself bring about an increase in human freedom, for technological developments threaten the structure of society, and society develops a proportionate number of restrictions to contain them. The automobile increases the speed and freedom of individual movement, and thereby brings a proportionate increase in police authority, with its complication of laws and penalties. In proportion as the production of retail goods becomes more efficient, the quality of craftsmanship and design decreases. The aeroplane facilitates travel, and therefore regiments travel: a modern traveller, processed through an immigration shed, might think ruefully of the contrast with Sterne, travelling to France in the eighteenth century, suddenly remembering that Britain was at war with France, and that consequently he would need his passport. The same principle affects science itself. The notion that science, left to itself, is bound to evolve more and more of the truth about the world is another illusion, for science can never exist outside a society, and that society, whether deliberately or unconsciously, directs its course. Still, the importance of keeping science 'free', i.e., unconsciously rather than deliberately directed, is immense. In the Soviet Union, and increasingly in America as well, science is allowed to develop 'freely' so that the political power can hijack its technological by-products. But this means a steady pressure on science to develop in the direction useful to that power: target-knowledge, as the Nazis called it. I am not saying that there are no answers to these questions: I am saying that no improvement in the human situation can take place independently of the human will to improve, and that confidence in automatic or impersonal improvement is always misplaced.

In earlier times the sense of alienation and anxiety was normally projected as the fear of hell, the 'too late' existence awaiting those who, as Dante's Virgil says, had never come alive. In our day this fear is attached, not to another world following this one, but to the future of our own world. The first half of the modern century was still full of progressive optimism: an unparalleled number of Utopias, or visions of a stabilized future, were written, and universal prosperity was widely predicted, partly because most of the people being exploited in the main centres of culture were well out of sight in Asia or Africa. After the midway point of 1917 there came an abrupt change. Spengler's *Decline of the West* appeared in Germany the next year. Here it is said that history consists of cultural developments which rise, mature, and decline like organisms. After they have exhausted their creative possibilities, they turn into 'civilizations'. The arts give place to technology and engineering; vast cities spread over the landscape, inhabited by uprooted masses of people, and dictatorships and annihilation wars become the course of history. A Classical 'culture' entered this stage with Alexander, and, later, the rise of Rome. The Western world entered it with Napoleon, and is now in the stage corresponding to that of the Punic Wars, with the great world states fighting it out for supremacy. Spengler is often dismissed as 'fatalistic' today, but his paralleling of our historical situation with earlier periods, especially that of the Roman Empire, and his point that our technology could be part of a decline as easily as it could be part of an advance, are conceptions that we all accept now, whether we realize it or not, as something which is inseparably part of our perspective.

The progressive belief suffered a rude set-back in America in the crash of 1929; it was adopted by the Soviet Union as part of its revolutionary world-view, but is gradually fading out even there, much as the expectation of the end of the world faded out of early Christian thought. In our day the Utopia has been succeeded by what is being called, by analogy, the 'dystopia', the nightmare of the future. H. G. Wells is a good example of a writer who built all his hopes around the myth of progress, in which the role of saviour was played by a self-evolving science. His last publication, however, *The Mind at the End of its Tether* (1940), carried all the furious bitterness of an outraged idealism. Orwell's *1984* is a better-known dystopia, and perhaps comes as close as any book to being the definitive *Inferno* of our time. It is a particularly searching study because of the way in which it illustrates how so many aspects of culture, including science, technology, history, and language, would operate in their demonic or perverted forms. The conception of progress took off originally from eighteenth-century discussions about the natural society, where the progressive view was urged by Bolingbroke and Rousseau and the opposite one by Swift and Burke. According to Rousseau, the natural and reasonable society of the future was buried underneath the accumulated injustices and absurdities of civilization, and all man had to do was to release it by revolution. Writers of our day have mostly reverted to the view of Swift's *Gulliver's Travels*, that slavery is to man at least as natural a state as freedom: this is the central insight of one of the most penetrating stories of our time, William Golding's *Lord of the Flies*, and is certainly implied, if not expressed, in Aldous Huxley's *Brave New World* and many similar works.

It is natural that many people should turn from the vision of such a world to some illusion or distracting fiction that seems to afford a more intelligible environment. Nationalism is or can be a distracting fiction of this kind. The nation, economically considered, is a form of private enterprise, a competing business in the world's market; hence, for most people, nationality comes to their attention chiefly through inconvenience —customs duties, income taxes, and the like. But it also may provide some sense of a protected place. It can't happen here, we may say, deliberately forgetting that the distinction between here and there has ceased to exist. It is significant that intense nationalism or regionalism today is a product either of resistance to or of disillusionment with progress. Progress, when optimistic, always promises some form of exodus from history as we know it, some emergence on to a new plateau of life. Thus the Marxist revolution promised deliverance from history as history had previously been, a series of class struggles. But just as there are neurotic individuals who cannot get beyond some blocking point in their emotional past, so there are neurotic social groups who feel a compulsion to return to a previous point in history, as Mississippi keeps fighting the Civil War over again, and some separatists in Quebec the British Conquest.

However, one wonders whether, in an emergency, this compulsion to return to the same point, the compulsion of Quixote to fight over again the battles he found in his books, is not universal in our world. In ordinary life, the democratic and Communist societies see each other as dystopias, their inhabitants hysterical and brainwashed by propaganda, identifying their future with what is really their destruction. Perhaps both sides, as Blake would say, become what they behold: in any case seeing tendencies to tyranny only on the other side is mere hypocrisy. The Nuremberg trials laid down the principle that man remains a free agent even in the worst of tyrannies, and is not only morally but legally responsible for resisting orders that outrage the conscience of mankind. The Americans took an active part in prosecuting these trials, but when America itself stumbled into the lemming-march horror of Vietnam the principle was forgotten and the same excuses and defiances reappeared.

All the social nightmares of our day seem to focus on some unending and inescapable form of mob rule. The most permanent kind of mob rule is not anarchy, nor is it the dictatorship that regularizes anarchy, nor even the imposed police state depicted by Orwell. It is rather the self-policing state, the society incapable of formulating an articulate criticism of itself and of developing a will to act in its light. This is a condition that we are closer to, on this continent, than we are to dictatorship. In such a society the conception of progress would reappear as a donkey's carrot, as the new freedom we shall have as soon as some regrettable temporary necessity is out of the way. No one would notice that the necessities never come to an end, because the communications media would have destroyed the memory.

The idea of progress, we said, is not really that of man progressing, but of man releasing forces that will progress by themselves. The root of the idea is the fact that science progressively develops its conception of the world. Science is a vision of nature which perceives the elements in nature that correspond to the reason and the sense of structure in the scientist's mind. If we look at our natural environment with different eyes, with emotion or desire or trying to see in it things that answer other needs than those of the reason, nature seems a vast unthinking indifference, with no evidence of meaning or purpose. In proportion as we have lost confidence in progress, the scientific vision of nature has tended to separate from a more imaginative and emotional one which regards nature or the human en- vironment as absurd or meaningless. The absurd is now one of the central elements in the contemporary myth, along with alienation and anxiety, and has extended from man's feeling about nature to his feeling about his own society. For society, like nature, has the power of life and death over us, yet has no real claim on our deeper loyalties. The absurdity of power is clearer in a democratic society, where we are deprived of the comforting illusions that surround royalty. In a de- mocracy no one pretends to identify the real form of society either with the machinery of business or with the machinery of government. But in that case where is the society to be found to which we do owe loyalty?

There are two contemporary plays which seem to sum up with peculiar vividness and forcefulness the malaise that I have described as the alienation of prog- ress. One is Beckett's *Waiting for Godot*. The main theme of this play is the paralysis of activity that is brought about by the dislocation of life in time, where there is no present, only a faint memory of a past, and an expectation of a future with no power to move towards it. Of the two characters whose dialogue forms most of the play, one calls himself Adam; at another time they identify themselves with Cain and Abel; at other times, vaguely and helplessly, with the thieves crucified with Christ. 'Have we no rights?' one asks. 'We got rid of them' the other says—distinctly, according to the stage direction. And even more explicitly: 'at this place, at this moment of time, all mankind is us.' They spend the whole action of the play waiting for a certain Godot to arrive: he never comes; they deny that they are 'tied' to him, but they have no will to break away. All that turns up is a Satanic figure called Pozzo, with a clown tied to him in a parody of their own state. On his second appearance Pozzo is blind, a condition which detaches him even further from time, for, he says, 'the blind have no notion of time'.

The other play is Albee's *Who's Afraid of Virginia Woolf?* The title of this play is echoed from the depression song, 'Who's afraid of the big bad wolf?', where the 'wolf' was a specific fear of unemployment. I began this talk by saying that the modern century was the first to study itself objectively, and that this has created an opposition between the active mind that struggles for reality and the passive mind that prefers to remain in an illusion. Art, culture, the imagination, are on the side of reality and activity: Virginia Woolf, chosen because of the sound of her last name, represents this side, and the characters are 'afraid' of her because they cannot live without illusion. The two men in the play are a historian and a scientist, facing the past and the future, both impotent in the present. 'When people can't abide things as they are,' says the historian George, 'when they can't abide the present, they do one of two things . . . either they turn to a contemplation of the past, as I have done, or they set about to alter the future.' But nobody in the play does either. George can murder his imaginary child, but the destruction of illusion does not bring him reality, for the only reality in his life was contained in the illusion which he denied.

I have tried to indicate the outlines of the picture that contemporary imagination has drawn of its world, a jigsaw-puzzle picture in which the Canada of 1967 is one of the pieces. It is a picture mainly of disillusionment and fear, and helps to explain why our feelings about our Centennial are more uneasy than they are jubilant. In the twentieth century most anniversaries, including the annual disseminating neurosis of Christmas, are touched with foreboding. I noticed this early in life, for my twenty-first birthday was spent at the Chicago World's Fair of 1933, entitled 'A Century of Progress', where the crowds were much more preoccupied with worrying about the depression than with celebrating what had led to it. And yet this picture, as I have tried also to explain, is the picture that the contemporary imagination draws of itself in a mirror. Looking into the mirror is the active mind which struggles for consistency and continuity of outlook, which preserves its memory of its past and clarifies its view of the present. Staring back at it is the frozen reflection of that mind, which has lost its sense of continuity by projecting it on some mechanical social process, and has found that it has also lost its dignity, its freedom, its creative power, and its sense of the present, with nothing left except a fearful apprehension of the future. The mind in the mirror, like the characters in Beckett, cannot move on its own initiative. But the more repugnant we find this reflection, the less likely we are to make the error of Narcissus, and identify ourselves with it. I want now to discuss the active role that the arts, more particularly literature, have taken in forming the contemporary imagination, which has given us this picture. The picture itself reflects anxiety, and as long as man is capable of anxiety he is capable of passing through it to a genuine human destiny.

2

Improved binoculars

LET US BEGIN by look-
ing at some of the characteristics that we generally
associate with the word 'modern', especially in the arts.
'Modern', in itself, means simply recent: in Shakespeare's day it meant mediocre, and it still sometimes
carries that meaning as an emotional overtone. In its
ordinary colloquial sense it implies an advanced state
of technology and the social attitudes of a highly urbanized life. In some Western Canadian towns, for example, houses with outdoor privies are advertised as 'un-
modern'. But 'modern' has also become a historical term

like 'Romantic', 'Baroque', or 'Renaissance'. It would be convenient if, like 'Romantic', the colloquial uses of the word were spelled in lower case and the cultural term with a capital, but this is not established. Like 'Romantic' again, 'modern' as a cultural term refers partly to a historical period, roughly the last century, but it is also partly a descriptive term, not a purely historical term like 'medieval'. Just as we feel that Keats or Byron are Romantic and that some of their contemporaries, Jane Austen for example, are either not Romantic at all or are less Romantic, so we feel that 'modern' is in part a style or attitude in recent culture, and that some of the artists and writers of the last century have been 'more modern' than others.

'Modern', so used, describes certain aspects of an international style in the arts which began, mainly in Paris, about a hundred years ago. Out of compliment to our centenary, I shall date it from 1867, the year of the death of Baudelaire. The larger context of this 'modern' is the series of vast changes that began to take place, not around 1867, but a century earlier. These earlier changes included the American and French revolutions, the beginning of the Industrial Revolution, new and more analytical schools of thought, such as the French Encyclopaedists and the British Utilitarians, and the cultural development we call Romantic. By 1867 this movement had entered on a second phase, continuous with but distinguishable from its predecessor, and this begins the modern century properly speaking. The thinkers Darwin and Marx, and later Freud and Frazer, the writers Rimbaud, Flaubert, Dostoevsky, and Nietzsche, the impressionist painters and their successors, belong to it.

During the whole of the last century, there has naturally been the most frantic resistance to 'modern' culture, for both the highbrow arts and the popular ones, though for different reasons, have a powerful capacity to stir up guilt feelings, personal insecurities, and class resentments. The Nazis called the modern style a Jewish conspiracy, the Jews being for them the symbols of a racism without a national boundary. The Communist hierarchy calls it an imperialistic conspiracy, and particularly attacks the 'formalism' which it asserts symbolizes the ideology of a decadent class. One may suspect from such things as the Sinyavsky-Daniel trial that the periodic 'thaws' in the Soviet Union are mainly a device to determine where the really dangerous threats to the bureaucracy are coming from, but even so they show something of the tremendous pressure building up against the barriers of official stupidity and panic, which may eventually break through them. Chinese resistance is still militant, though of course the cultural traditions there are different. Hysterical people in the democracies, in their turn, call the modern style a Communist conspiracy; in Canada it is often called Americanization. It is true that many aspects of modern culture, especially popular culture, are of American origin, like jazz, but America is a province conquered by the international modern much more than it is a source of it.

In literature, the international character of the modern style has been partly disguised by difference in language. Just as we seem to be moving into a world in which we meet the same kind of things everywhere, from hydro installations to Beatle haircuts, so we seem to be moving into a world in which English will become either the first or the second language of practically everybody. But of course it does not follow that English or any other language will become a world *literary* language. The last hundred years have also been a period in which many minority languages have been maintained, revived, or in some cases practically invented, by an intense regional patriotism. Hebrew, Norwegian, Flemish, Irish, and French in Canada are examples. The prestige of such movements is one of several elements that have helped to shape a common view which is the opposite of the one I am advancing here. Culture, it is often said, in contrast to economic and political developments, is local, regional, and decentralized, as dependent on an immediate environment as a fine wine or a delicate and traditional handicraft like peasant costumes. The first step in the creation of an indigenous culture, therefore, is a firm boundary line, and the next step is the cultural equivalent of high tariffs against foreign influences.

This theory of culture probably originated in Romantic theories about a creative 'folk', and has been confusing the Canadian scene for even longer than the past hundred years. I held a version of it myself, or thought I did, when I was beginning to write in Canadian periodicals a generation ago. According to Shelley in his preface to *Prometheus Unbound*, the decentralizing of Great Britain into a dozen or more districts, each with its own cultural centre, would help to awaken the country to the kind of cultural vitality enjoyed earlier by such small towns as Periclean Athens or Medicean Florence. It sounds unlikely, but it is a roughly consistent extension of Shelley's association of human freedom with the self-determining of national cultures, particularly Greece and Italy. William Morris, again, thought of culture as essentially 'manufacture' in the strict sense, as the work of brain and hand which has a totally different function from that of mechanized industry. Hence his ideal world is one of small and relatively isolated communities, governing themselves by local councils and keeping themselves busy making things. In his view the so-called minor or useful arts are the index of a culture; the major arts are assimilated to them, and both are produced by a domestic economy. In T. S. Eliot, again, we find 'culture' associated with an intense decentralization. Eliot's *Notes Toward a Definition of Culture* and similar essays are much preoccupied with Welsh and Scottish nationalisms and with the desirability of having most people not move from the place where they were born.

The attempts to 'purify' a language are also part of the resistance to the international modern. It is consistent with William Morris's attitude that he should deplore the mongrel nature of modern English which has helped to make it a world language, its grafting of so many Latin conceptual and Greek technical terms on a Teutonic stock. Morris was one of those who wanted

English to throw out its load of loan words and return to more Teutonic methods of making up a vocabulary, such as calling a market a cheaping place or a baby carriage a pushwainling. Such efforts got nowhere in English, but some other languages, such as Persian, or German in the Nazi period, were more successful in driving out foreign influences on vocabulary and syntax, at least for a time. Even in Australia, I understand, there has been a group of poets devoted to putting as many native Australian words into their poems as possible. A late echo of this tendency is the anti-'joual' campaign in French Canada, the effort to set up European French as a standard of correctness against the normal linguistic developments which tend to Anglicize and Americanize French Canadian speech. Outside literature, resistance to the modern style has very little if anything to put in its place. Approved Nazi painting and approved Communist fiction can only fall back on idioms derived from the art before 1867, on worn-out Romantic and Victorian formulas which can no longer be used with their original energy and conviction. If we compare T. S. Eliot's theories about decentralized culture with his own poetry and the quality of his influence, both of which are completely international, it is clear that the theories are merely something dreamed up, and have no relation to any cultural facts.

It is of course true that a coherent environment is a cultural necessity. And many of the world's great cultural developments do seem to have been assisted by some kind of local resistance to imperial expansion. The

catalyzer of ancient Greek culture was clearly the successful battle for independence by a province on the
fringes of what was essentially, in its civilization, a
Persian world. Hebrew culture drew a similar strength
from its resistance to Egyptian and Mesopotamian imperialism. Elizabethan England and seventeenth-century
Holland were provincial rebels against the centralizing
forces of the Papacy and the Hapsburg Empire; Germany in the Napoleonic period and, on a smaller scale,
Ireland at the turn of this century joined a cultural
efflorescence to a political resistance. In our day similar
movements are going on, though more confined to the
cultural area. The liberalizing of Communist culture is
much more likely to start in Poland or Hungary than in
the Soviet Union, and Mexico has maintained a remarkable cultural independence of its northern neighbour.
The feeling that Canada in this respect has left undone
what it ought to have done amounts to a national neurosis. But what I have described is not a social law: it is
merely something that often happens, and just as often
fails to happen. And even if it were a social law, there
are many elements in Canada's situation that would
make the applying of it to Canada a false analogy.

Even apart from this, however, there is still the question: where does the seed come from that grows up in
these localities of provincial resistance? Spontaneous
generation is no more credible in culture than it is in
biology. Seeds of culture can only come from the centres of civilization which are already established, often
those centres against which the local culture is revolt-

ing. As I have tried to show elsewhere, the forms of art are autonomous: poems and pictures are born out of earlier poems and pictures, not out of new localities, and novelty of content or experience in such localities cannot produce originality of form. We notice that the more popular an aspect of culture is, such as jazz music, films, or the kind of poetry associated with beatnik and similar groups, the more quickly it becomes international in its idiom. To try to found a serious culture in Canada on a middle-class intellectual resistance to popular culture of this kind would be the last word in futility. All this may seem too obvious now to insist on, but many intellectuals, in both English and French parts of the country, have in the past been engaged in an inglorious rearguard action of trying to encourage a regional or tourist's-souvenir literature, and it is perhaps still worth repeating that the practice is useless and the theory mistaken. Complete immersion in the international style is a primary cultural requirement, especially for countries whose cultural traditions have been formed since 1867, like ours. Anything distinctive that develops within the Canadian environment can only grow out of participation in this style.

The distinctively 'modern' element in the culture of the last century has played, and continues to play, a revolutionary role in society. It may be easiest to illustrate this from the pictorial arts. In medieval painting the prevailing conventions were religious, and for that and many other reasons the technique of representation was highly stylized. As the centuries went on, we can

see a growing realism in the painting which, in its historical context, was an emancipating force. The Byzantine type of stylizing comes to be thought stiff and
angular; lighter and springier lines succeed in later
Gothic; more human touches appear in the divine faces;
landscapes sprout and blossom in the background; an
occasional nude appears if the iconography makes it possible, as in pictures of St Sebastian or Mary Magdalene.
The growth of realism, in other words, is also a growth
in the humanizing of the projected myths, man recover-
ing for himself the forms he had created.

As we pass into the Renaissance, and painting becomes more secularized, it begins to reflect something
of the spirit that is also in Renaissance science, the feeling of man as a subject confronting an objective world.
With the development of perspective the pictorial vision
settled on a fixed point in space. As a result there grew
up some curiously pedantic critical theories of painting,
which assumed that it was primarily a representational
art, and that the function of painting was not to create
a vision but to record one. The Elizabethan critic Putten-
ham, writing in the age of Michelangelo and Titian,
even asserted that the painter had no creative power at
all, but merely imitated nature in the same way that an
ape imitates a man. This dreary doctrine found its way
into Shakespeare's *Winter's Tale*, somewhat disguised.
I mention it only to emphasize the fact it misunder-
stands, which is the tremendous projecting force in
Renaissance and Baroque painting. In Rubens, the great
spiralling and twisting rhythms, usually starting from

a diagonal, that, so to speak, pick up the eye and hurl it into the furthest point of the picture, express a kind of will to objectify. The same kind of will is also in Rembrandt, in a quieter and more contemplative form, as the eye is led to the points of light that emerge from the graduated shadows. Rembrandt carried this objectified form of painting about as far as human skill could carry it, and imposed his way of seeing on successors for generations.

When we look at the later work of Turner, contemporary with the great English Romantic poets, there is a different feeling which, in the particular context we are speaking of now, might be called a colossal emancipation of vision. It is not the titles of such pictures as 'Rain, Steam and Speed' that make us feel that we are in a new world, but the sense of a new way of seeing. We are not looking *at* nature here, but are identified with the processes and powers of nature, the creative forces symbolized by the swirling colours, the dissolving shapes, and the expanding perspective where we seem to see everything at once, as though the eye were surrounding the picture. This is imitating nature as the Romantic age conceived imitation, where man and nature are thought of as connected, not by the subject-object relation of consciousness, but by an identity of process, man being a product of the organic power of nature. As Coleridge says, it is this latter, the *natura naturans*, that the painter imitates, not the structure of *natura naturata* in front of him. With the great impressionists who followed Turner the realistic tendency achieves a second culmination. Impressionism portrays, not a separated objective world that man contemplates, but a world of power and force and movement which is in man also, and emerges in the consciousness of the painter. Monet, painting Rouen cathedral in every aspect of light and shade, Renoir making the shapes in nature explode into vibrations of colour, Degas recording the poses of a ballet, are working in a world where objects have become events, and where time is a dimension of sense experience. We can, of course, look back on earlier painters and see the same things in Rubens or Tintoretto, but we see them there with the hindsight that impressionism has given us.

In all these centuries the representational aspect of painting is the organically growing aspect, the liberalizing force, the avant-garde movement. It is a realism of form, and as it develops it tends to become something of a conservative social force. Thus Dutch realism often reflects a quiet satisfaction in middle-class Dutch life, and in some modern painters—I think particularly of Vuillard— the visual aspect of our social experience is similarly bathed in a benevolent glow of beauty and charm. There is nothing wrong with this, but it was inevitable that there should also develop, as part of the expanding horizon of pictorial experience, a revolutionary or prophetic realism, of the sort that runs through Brueghel, Hogarth, Goya, and Daumier. This kind of realism is often not realistic in form: it may be presented as fantasy, as in Brueghel's 'Mad Margaret' or Goya's 'Caprichos'. But it tears apart the façade of society and shows us the forces working behind that façade, and is realistic in the sense of sharpening our vision of society as a mode of existence rather than simply as an environment.

By 1867 impressionism was reaching its climax of development, and the 'modern' world was taking shape. But there are very different elements in the modern world which are also making pictorial impressions. In advertising, propaganda, and a great deal of mass culture, of the type I referred to in my previous lecture, and which is usually intended to be received passively, the prevailing idiom is one that may be called stupid realism. By stupid realism I mean what is actually a kind of sentimental idealism, an attempt to present a conventionally attractive or impressive appearance as an actual or attainable reality. Thus it is a kind of parody or direct counter-presentation to prophetic realism. We see it in the vacuous pretty-girl faces of advertising, in the clean-limbed athletes of propaganda magazines, in the haughty narcissism of shop-window mannequins, in the heroically transcended woes of soap-opera heroines, in eulogistic accounts of the lives of celebrities, usually those in entertainment, in the creation by Madison Avenue of a wise and kindly father-figure out of some political stooge, and so on. The 'social realism' of Communism, though much better in theory than this, has in practice much in common with it. It seems clear that an officially approved realism cannot carry on the revolutionary tradition of Goya and Daumier. It is not anti-Communism that makes us feel

61

that the disapproved writers, Daniel and Babel and Pasternak, have most to say to us: on the contrary, it is precisely such writers who best convey the sense of Russians as fellow human beings, caught in the same dilemmas that we are. Revolutionary realism is a questioning, exploring, searching, disturbing force: it cannot go over to established authority and defend the fictions which may be essential to authority, but are never real. We may compare in American painting the lively development of the so-called ashcan school with the WPA murals in post offices which glumly rehearsed the progress of transportation from camel to jeep, and which are now mostly covered up.

In this context we can see that realism of form has changed sides: it is no longer a liberalizing and emancipating force, incorporating the hopes and fears of humanity into the icons demanded by churches, public buildings, and well-to-do patrons. The projected image is now the weapon of the enemy, and consequently it is the power to project the image that becomes liberalizing. A new kind of energy is released in the painting that followed the impressionists, an energy which concentrates on the sheer imaginative act of painting in itself, on painting as the revolt of the brain behind the eye against passive sensation. Cézanne is the hinge on which this more specifically 'modern' movement turns, but it has of course taken a great variety of forms since. One is the abstraction, or abstract expressionism later, which portrays the combination of form and colour without reference to representation. Another is the action-painting which tries to communicate the sense of process and growth in the act of painting. Still another is the 'pop art' which presents the projected images of stupid realism itself, in a context where the critical consciousness is compelled to make an active response to them.

Stupid realism depends for its effect on evoking the ghost of a dead tradition: it is a parody of the realism which was organic a century or two ago. The active and revolutionary element in painting today is the element of formalism. (I know that I am using 'formalism' in a looser sense than it is used in Marxist criticism, but I am trying to suggest some of the wider implications of the contrasting views.) I said that to the painters of the age of Giotto the old Byzantine conventions were beginning to seem unnecessarily constricting. But in the stupid realism of commercial late Roman sculpture, with its stodgy busts and sarcophagi, the sharp angular patterns of Byzantine leap out with a clean and vital flame. The cycle of culture has turned once more, and once again it is the stylized that is the emancipating force. Of course there is always a central place for a realism which is not stupid, which continues to sharpen our vision of the world and the society that are actually there. But the exhilarating sense of energy in great formalism is so strong that modern realism tends to express itself in formalist conventions. In Brueghel's 'Slaughter of the Innocents' a conventional religious subject is located in a realistic landscape that recalls the terror and misery of sixteenth-century Flanders; in

Picasso's 'Guernica' the terror and misery of twentieth-century Spain is expressed with the stylizing intensity of a religious primitivism.

In literature there is a change from Romantic to modern around 1867 that is in some respects even sharper and more dramatic than the shift from impressionism to Cézanne. At the beginning of the Romantic period around 1800, an increased energy of propulsion had begun to make itself felt, an energy that often suggests something mechanical. When the eighteenth-century American composer Billings developed contrapuntal hymn-settings which he called 'fuguing-tunes', he remarked that they would be 'more than twenty times as powerful as the old slow tunes'. The quantitative comparison, the engineering metaphor, the emphasis on speed and power, indicate a new kind of sensibility already present in pre-Revolutionary and pre-industrial America. Much greater music than his is touched by the same feeling: the finale of Mozart's Linz Symphony in c is based on the bodily rhythm of the dance, but the finale of the Beethoven Rasoumovsky Quartet in the same key foreshadows the world of the express train. Bernard Shaw compares the finale of Beethoven's opus 106 to the dance of atoms in the molecule, whatever that sounds like. A similar propulsive movement makes itself felt in those greatly misunderstood poems of Wordsworth, 'The Idiot Boy', 'Peter Bell', 'The Waggoner', where we also have references to 'flying boats' and the like, and in many poems of Shelley, where again some of the characters seem to be operating

private hydroplanes, like the Witch of Atlas. This sense
of the exhilaration of mechanical movement continues
into the modern period, especially in the Italian Futurist
movement around the time of the First World War. In
fact the modern is often popularly supposed to be primarily a matter of 'streamlining', of suggesting in fur-
niture and building, as well as in the formal arts themselves, the clean, spare, economical, functional lines of
a swiftly moving vehicle.

But in modern literature at least, especially poetry,
we have to take account of other tendencies. The decline of admiration for continuity is one of the most
striking differences between the Romantic and the
modern feeling. It perhaps corresponds to the decline
of confidence in progress that we discussed earlier.
The Swinburne whose linear energy carries his reader
through hundreds of pages of poetic dramas and lyrics
is felt, by Eliot, to be a poet 'who does not think', as
less modern in both feeling and technique than the
Hopkins who prefers the techniques of 'sprung' to those
of 'running' rhythm. (Swinburne is more correctly esti-
mated now, but as part of a critical development which
has outgrown the anti-Romantic phase of modernism,
and has got its sense of tradition in better focus.) In
France, one modern poet even maintained that the function of poetry was to wring the neck of rhetoric. Such
a poet would be bound to accept the dictum of Poe, a
most influential one in the modern period, that a long
poem is really a contradiction in terms, for it is rhetoric,
in the sense of a conventional form of expression that

supplies a continuous verbal texture, which makes a poem long. In French literature this rhetorical continuity is associated particularly with Victor Hugo, who is thought of as a pre-modern Romantic. Modern poetry tends to be discontinuous, to break the hypnotic continuity of a settled metre, an organizing narrative, or a line of thought, all of which, it is felt, are apt to move too far in the direction of passive response. In Eliot's *The Waste Land* the scenes, episodes, and quoted lines are stuck into the reader's mind somewhat as the slogans and illustrations of advertising are—tachistoscopically, as the educators say. But, once there, the reader is compelled to a creative act of putting the fragments together. The continuity of the poem, in short, has been handed over to him.

One may see here a tendency parallel to the formalism of modern painting. What corresponds for the ear to stupid realism in the visual arts is partly rhetoric, in the sense used above, the surrounding of an advertised object with emotional and imaginative intensity, the earnest, persuasive voice of the radio commercial, the torrent of prefabricated phrases and clichés in political oratory. Nineteenth-century social critics who could not always distinguish the paranoid from the prophetic, such as Carlyle and Ruskin, often work themselves up emotionally by means of rhetoric into states of mind where they are possessed by the rhetoric and are no longer controlling it, so that a certain automatism comes into the writing. We see this also in a debased form in propaganda harangues. In general, uncontrolled rhetorical babble is an expression of a sado-masochist cycle, where the thing that is uncontrolled is a desire either to hurt someone else or to humiliate oneself. The definitive presentation of the 'anti-hero' in modern literature, Dostoevsky's *Notes from Underground*, emphasizes this feature of uncontrolled mechanical talk, and traces it to an excess of conscious awareness over the power of action. The narrator despises himself, and yet admires himself for being honest enough to despise himself, and hence is continually possessed by rhetorical rages directed either at himself or at some projection of himself. Similar tendencies exist in Shakespeare's Hamlet, which is the chief reason why Hamlet, with his melancholy and his broken power of decision, his self-accusations and his uncontrolled brutality to others, becomes so central a Romantic and modern image of consciousness. The anti-rhetorical tendency in modern literature is part of a general tendency in modern culture to plant a series of anti-tank traps, so to speak, in the way of the rumbling and creaking invaders of our minds.

In the creation of poetry there seems to be an oddly paradoxical element. Something oracular, something that holds and charms and spellbinds, is involved in it, and the oracular permits no distraction or criticism: nothing must dispel its mood. Yet what the oracle expresses is frequently an epigram, a pun, an ambiguous statement, or a conundrum that sounds like a bad joke, like the witches' elliptical prophecies to Macbeth. Wit is addressed to the awakened critical intelligence and to a perception of the incongruous. Poetry has often veered between these two aspects of the poetic process: in the age of Pope, wit was the preferred element; with the Romantics a more solemnly oracular tone dominated, or alternated with wit, as in Byron. In the modern period the prevailing tone tended to shift again to wit. The degree of abstraction in painting that we see in Léger or Modigliani, or perhaps even in Cubism, where a representational picture has been assimilated to geometrical outlines, is witty, in somewhat the same way that poetry stepping along in antithetical rhyming couplets is witty. In both it is the *discordia concors* of artistic discipline and natural untidiness that evokes the sense of wit, as when a woman's breast becomes a sphere or an epigram falls neatly into ten iambic syllables. T. E. Hulme, Wyndham Lewis, and others, in the early anti-Romantic phase of modernism, were much struck by this analogy between abstraction and satirical wit, and set it up as a standard against the continuous rhetoric and oracular solemnity that they found in the Romantics, from Wordsworth to Gertrude Stein. Of poets, perhaps Auden in English has given us most clearly the sense of creation as play, an expression of man as *homo ludens*. The contrived and artificial patterns of his verse are consistent with this, just as the light verse they resemble is more contrived than heavy verse, and play-novels like detective stories more contrived than 'serious' fiction. Valéry's view of poetry as a game bound by arbitrary rules like chess is similar, and Valéry remarks that 'inspiration' is a state of mind in the reader, not in the writer—another example of the modern tendency to turn as much activity as possible over to the reader.

There are many complaints about the obscurity of the arts in the modern world, and about the indifference that the modern artist seems to have for his public. But we can see by now that modern art is directly involved in a militant situation peculiar to our time. It does not simply come into being as an expression of human creative power: it is born on a battlefield, where the enemies are the anti-arts of passive impression. In this context the arts demand an active response with an intensity that hardly existed before. Hence the modern artist is actually in an immediate personal relation with his reader or viewer: he throws the ball to him, so to speak, and his art depends on its being caught at the other end. We have already noticed how in *The Waste Land* (and much other modern poetry) the poet hands the continuity of his poem over to the reader, and one could make out a very good case for saying that the reader of *Finnegans Wake* is the hero of that book, the person who laboriously spells out the message of the dream. *Finnegans Wake* belongs of course to the stream-of-consciousness technique in modern fiction. This technique, which is still going strong in the novels of Samuel Beckett, is continuous, but not rhetorically continuous: that is, the links are associative and not merely ready-made as they are in a propagandist speech, hence they require an active reader to see the sequential logic in them.

One would expect to find in the modern, then, some decline in the prestige of the particular quality in art represented by the term 'craftsmanship', or, perhaps more accurately, by the highly significant epithet 'finished'. The work of art is traditionally something set up to be admired: it is placed in a hierarchy where the 'classic' or 'masterpiece' of perfect form is at the top. Modern art, especially in such developments as action-painting, is concerned to give the impression of process rather than product, of something emerging out of the heat of struggle and still showing the strain of its passing from conception to birth. Balzac tells a celebrated story about a painter whose masterpiece broke down into a tangle of meaningless lines. But the modern century has to take this parable of the *chef d'oeuvre inconnu* seriously, for the lines are not meaningless if they record the painter's involvement with his subject and also demand ours. Malraux has remarked how much the sketch, the sense of something rapidly blocked out and left incomplete, seems to us the index of an artist's vitality. The same principles hold for poetry, even to the extent that a poet today can get more money out of selling his manuscript excreta to libraries than he can out of royalties on the published volume. Dramatists try to break up the hypnotic illusion of the play by various devices that suggest a dramatic process in formation, such as introducing stagehands or prompters, or breaking down the distinction between actor and role. Such devices are regarded by Brecht as a creative form of alienation, giving the audience a closer view of imaginative reality by chopping holes in the rhetorical façade. Novelists adopt similar devices to break the story-teller's spell on the reader: thus Gide's *The Counterfeiters* is a story about a novelist writing a novel called *The Counterfeiters*. Readers of Canadian literature may see similar tendencies in Reaney's *Listen to the Wind* or Leonard Cohen's *Beautiful Losers*.

The tendency to prefer the imperfect work engaged in history to the perfected masterpiece that pulls away from time is closely related to another tendency which also originates in the opposition to passive anti-art. Advertising and propaganda are interested arts, arts with ulterior motives. Behind them is a course of action which they end by exhorting one to follow. A good deal of literature has followed the same pattern (e.g., *The Pilgrim's Progress*, *Self-Help* by Samuel Smiles) and still does. But as a rule the work of art as such is disinterested: there is nothing beyond itself to which it points as the fulfilment of itself. In modern painting and poetry, especially in the last two decades, there has been a good deal of emphasis not only on this disinterested and self-containing aspect of the arts, but of attack on those tendencies within the arts themselves that seem to lead us passively on from one thing to another. A detective story is a good example of this donkey's-carrot writing: we begin it to find out what we are told on the last page. Writing with this structure is teleological: it contains a hidden purpose, and we read on to discover what that purpose is.

Many modern poets, with William Carlos Williams

at their head, regard such concealing of a hidden design
as gimmick-writing: for them, the image, the scene, the
thing presented, the immediate experience, *is* the reality
that the arts are concerned with, and to go beyond this
is to risk dishonesty. The theory of the modern style
in poetry is set out in the letters of Rimbaud known as
the *lettres du voyant*, with their insistence that the
genuine poet sees directly, in contrast to the rhetori-
cian who talks about what he sees. The same kind of
emphasis has been common in painting for a long time:
music has been affected by it more recently, but perhaps more radically than any other art. Classical music,
up to quite recent times, has been intensely teleological:
in symphonies from Haydn to Brahms we feel strongly
how the end of a movement is implied in the beginning,
and how we are led towards it step by step. In much
contemporary music, both electronic and conventional,
the emphasis is on the immediate sense impression of
sound: the music is not going anywhere; it may even
be proceeding by chance, as in some of the experiments
of John Cage. The ear is not thrown forward into the
future, to hear a theme being worked out or a discord
resolved: it is kept sternly in the present moment. This
conception of the unit of experience as a thing in itself
is of course an intensely impersonal attitude to art: the
writer (and similarly with the other arts) is doing all
he can to avoid the sense of impressing himself on
his reader by suggesting meaning or form or purpose
beyond what is presented. In this conception of *cho-
sisme*, as it is sometimes called, it is not simply con-

tinuity, but significance or meaning itself, which has been handed over to the reader.

One may see in most of these modern tendencies a good deal of distrust in the rational consciousness as the main area of communication in the arts. Modern art is irrational in many respects, but it is important to see why and in what ways it is. We spoke of advertising and propaganda as stunning or demoralizing the critical consciousness in order to move past it and set up their structures in the rest of the mind. There is clearly no point in setting the artists to defend a Maginot line that has already been outflanked: the artist has to move directly back into the attacked area, and set up his own structures there instead. Hence the various Freud-inspired movements, like surrealism, which communicate on a normally repressed level; hence too the great variety of modern developments of fantasy and articulated dream, where there is no identity, and where the world is like that of Milton's chaos, with things forming and disappearing by chance and melting into other things. In Kafka, for example, the event, the ordinary unit of a story, is replaced by the psychological event, and the social and other significances of what is happening are allegories of these psychological events. The primary emphasis is on the mental attitude that makes the events possible. Thus *The Castle* is presented as a kind of anxiety-nightmare, yet a theological allegory of God's dealings with man and a political allegory of the police state run in counterpoint with it.

I am not trying to suggest that all these modern tend-

encies form part of a single consistent pattern: far from
it. All that they have in common is an imaginative
opposition to the anti-arts of persuasion and exhorta-
tion. The obvious question to ask is, of course: granted
that the arts in the modern world are full of antagonism
to the anti-arts, granted that they parody them in all
sorts of clever ways, granted that they encourage an
active instead of a passive response, does this really
make them socially effective? In a world resounding
every day with the triumphs of slanted news and brainwashed politics, what can poetry and painting do, tor-
toises in a race with hares? This question is one of the
most powerful arguments of our enemy the accuser.
We are constantly learning from the alienation of progress that merely trying to clarify one's mind is useless
and selfish, because the individual counts for so little
in society. Marxism, with its carefully planned agenda
of revolution, provides the most complete answer to
the question: 'What then must we do?' The democracies provide more limited and piecemeal forms of
social activism, demonstrations, sit-ins, teach-ins, pro-
test marches, petitions and the like, partly (if one may
say so with all due sympathy and respect) as gestures
of homage to the superior effectiveness to be found in
the world of public relations and controversies. Similarly, the artist often feels an impulse to guarantee his
vision by his life, and hence we find the pattern of antagonism of art to anti-art repeated in an antagonism of
artist to society.

In political thought there is a useful fiction known

as the social contract, the sense that man enters into a certain social context by the act of getting born. In earlier contract theories, like that of Hobbes, the contract was thought of as universal, binding everyone without exception. From Rousseau on there is more of a tendency to divide people into those who accept and defend the existing social contract because they benefit from it, and the people who are excluded from most of its benefits, and so feel no obligation, or much less, to it. As everyone knows, Marx defined the excluded body as the proletariat or workers, and saw it as the means to a reconstituted society. Those who accept and are loyal to the social contract are known consistently, throughout the whole period, as the bourgeoisie or middle class, otherwise known, in different contexts, as Philistines or squares. Whenever artists think of themselves as a social group, they seem inclined to define themselves in terms of their opposition to the bourgeois society of the contract, with its materialistic and conformist standards.

Some of them have followed the Marxist form of this opposition, though very few in the English-speaking countries, and very few even of those have been of a type that under a proletarian dictatorship would survive the first purge. Radical sympathies in American fiction have tended rather to take the form of a sentimental populism, of a the-people-keep-marching-on type. During the depression, the contest of labour and management began to assume something of the dimensions of a revolution, and the labour movement still had, like the

Negroes today, the dignity of an oppressed group. As a result there was a considerable infiltration of working-class sympathies into the drama, films, and musical comedies of that period. But today few areas of American life are less inspiring to the Muse than the trade unions. The collapse of Communist sympathies in American culture was not the result of McCarthyism and other witch-hunts, which were not a cause but an effect of that collapse. The object of the witch-hunt is the witch, that is, a helpless old woman whose dangerousness is assumed to rationalize quite different interests and pleasures. Similarly the Communist issue in McCarthyism was a red herring for a democratic development of the big lie as a normal political weapon: if internal Communism had been a genuine danger the struggle against it would have taken a genuine form. Sympathy with Communism collapsed under the feeling that, even at its best, and ignoring its atrocities, the bureaucracy of Communism was enforcing much the same kind of social contract as the managerial and authoritarian elements in the democracies. Hence American liberals, even radicals, soon lost all faith in the moral superiority of Communism. Losing the faith was undoubtedly right: the immense relief with which they lost it may have been less so.

But if the Marxist form of radicalism, of the kind that helps to shape the dramas of Brecht and Gorky, is rare in American literature, there is a type of anarchism in it which is far more common. The figure of the individual who will not play the silly games of society, who seems utterly insignificant but represents an unbreak-able human force, runs through its literature from Rip van Winkle and the romances of Cooper to the present day. The patron saint of this tendency is Thoreau, re-treating to Walden to build his own cabin and assert that the only genuine America is the society of those who will not throw all their energies into the endless vacuum suction of imperialist hysteria and of consum-ing consumer goods. Huck Finn, drifting down the great river with Jim and preferring hell with Jim to the white slave-owner's heaven, is a similar figure, one of the bums, hoboes, and social outcasts who reach a deeper level of community than the rest of us. This outcast or hobo figure is the hero of most of the Chaplin films; he also finds a congenial haven in comic strips. The juvenile delinquent or emotionally disturbed adolescent may in some contexts be one of his contemporary equivalents, like the narrator of *The Catcher in the Rye*. Sympathy for the youth who sees no moral difference between delinquency and conformity still inspires such Utopian works as Paul Goodman's *Growing Up Absurd*. An earlier and very remarkable Canadian work of this anarchist kind is Frederick Philip Grove's *A Search for America*, where the America that the narrator searches for is again the submerged community that only the outcast experiences.

This form of proletariat has recently combined with another tradition of very different origin. One distinc-tively modern element in our culture, introduced in the main by the Romantic movement, is the conception of the serious writer, who is in a prophetic relation to society, and consequently in opposition to it. It is no longer sufficient to say, as Samuel Johnson did, that they who live to please must please to live: the serious writer is committed to saying what may not and probably will not please, even if he hopes to please enough, on a different level of pleasure, to be able to live also. With Baudelaire and his successors this antagonism to society becomes a way of life, usually called Bohemian, the antagonism being expressed partly in the over-simplifying phrase, *épater le bourgeois*. More accurately, the artist explores forbidden or disapproved modes of life in both imagination and experience. The square, the man who lives by the social contract, takes the public appearance of society to be, for him, its reality. Hence his obsessive tendency to appear in public clean, clothed, sober and accompanied by his wife. The artist may symbolize a more intensely imaginative community through dirt or slovenliness, lousifying himself as much as possible, as Rimbaud remarked, or through more openly acknowledged forms of sexual relationship outside marriage. Drugs and narcotics have been associated with the arts for a long time, but took on a new intensity and relevance to the creative process with the Romantic movement. The bourgeois view that the appearance of society is its reality is of course based on illusion, and we have seen how a breakdown in illusion is often more disturbing than genuine dangers. Similarly long hair in young men or pictures portraying a consenting sex act may stir up deeper social anxieties than actual delinquency or rape.

The combination of Bohemian and hobo traditions in the beat, hip, and other disaffected movements of our time seems to be part of an unconscious effort to define a social proletariat in Freudian instead of Marxist terms. Such groups find, or say they find, that a withdrawal from the social establishment is a necessary step in freeing them from repression and in releasing their creative energies. Creation is close to the sexual instinct, and it is in their attitude to sex that the two groups collide most violently, as each regards the other's views of sex as obscene. The Freudian proletarian sees established society as a repressive anxiety-structure, the basis of which is the effort to control the sexual impulse and restrict it to predictable forms of expression. His emphasis on the sexual aspect of life, his intense awareness of the role of the thwarted sexual drive in the cruelties and fears of organized society, make him quite as much a moralist as his opponent, though his moral aim is of course to weaken the anxiety-structure by the shock tactics of 'bad' words, pornography, or the publicizing of sexual perversions and deviations. The collision of youth and age is more openly involved in this kind of movement than elsewhere. In a society dominated by the alienation of progress, the young, whose lives are thrown forward to the future, achieve a curious kind of moral advantage, as though the continued survival of anyone whose life is mainly in the past required some form of justification. Certain other elements in this social movement, such as the growth of confessional and self-analysing groups, show some parallels with Marxist techniques.

The picaresque heroes of Kerouac are 'Dharma bums', social outcasts with serious social and even religious ideals. Their environment is the squalid and seedy urban one, the city that is steadily devouring the countryside, yet in their repudiation of everything structured and organized in it they struggle for an innocence that is almost pastoral. They seek a kinship with the nature which, like them, has been repressed, almost obliterated, by organized society. In two writers who have strongly influenced this Freudian proletariat movement, Henry Miller and D. H. Lawrence, pastoralism is a central theme. In the nineteenth century the relation of country to city was often thought of, in writers who had begun to hate and fear the rise of a metropolitan civilization, as a relation of innocence to experience, of the healthy natural virtues of the country corrupted by the feverish excitements of the town. This myth produced a good deal of nineteenth-century literature and social propaganda, ranging in value from Wordsworth's *Michael* to temperance melodramas. The pronouncements on drinking and sexual mores made by those in our society who are most spectacularly not with it, like many members of the lower clergy and the higher judiciary, are still often inspired by such visions of a virtuous rustic daring to be a Daniel in a wicked Babylon.

A number of other writers who continued the tradition of eighteenth-century primitivism also nurtured a tangled garden of metaphors about the need for being 'rooted in the soil', as part of a similar opposition to the metropolitan development of society. This form of *nostalgie de la boue* was a strong influence on nine-teenth-century fiction (Jean Giono, Knut Hamsun), though the ponderous prose lyrics it tended to specialize in are largely forgotten now. It is an attitude with a naturally strong bias toward racism, and in this form it entered into the *Völkisch* developments in Germany which lay behind much of Nazism. Nineteenth-century French Canada also had its propagandists for the motto *emparons-nous du sol*, idealizing the simple peasant bound to his land and his ancestral faith, a picture with a strong resemblance to Millet's 'Angelus', of which the most famous expression is *Maria Chapdelaine*. There were similar movements elsewhere in America, like the Southern agrarian movement of a generation ago. In Miller and Lawrence this pastoral theme is less senti-mentalized and more closely connected with the more deeply traditional elements of the pastoral: spontaneity in human relations, especially sexual relations; the stimulus to creative power that is gained from a simpler society, less obsessed by satisfying imaginary wants; and, at least in Lawrence, a sense of identity with nature of great delicacy and precision.

The pastoral withdrawal from bourgeois values merges insensibly into another, the sense of the artist as belonging to an élite or neo-aristocracy. The origin of this attitude is the feeling that in a world full of the panic of change, the artist's role is to make himself a

symbol of tradition, a sentinel or witness to the genuine
continuity in human life, like the London churches in
The Waste Land. In religion this attitude expresses itself, as a rule, in adherence or conversion to the Catholic
Church. Here it is often the Church as a symbol of
authority or tradition that is the attraction: Charles
Maurras expressed this most bluntly by saying that he
was interested in Catholicism but not in Christianity.
Political preferences are right-wing, with emphasis on
the traditional functions of aristocracy and royalty,
especially among those who actually were of aristo-
cratic origin, like Villiers de l'Isle Adam. Eliot's char-
acterizing of himself as 'royalist in politics' is a late and
not very resonant British echo of what was mainly a
French and nineteenth-century tendency. Economic preferences vary, but are always strongly against the con-
spiracies of international finance. In the twenties and
thirties many of this group were attracted to fascism,
which they saw as leading to a new recognition of
heroic energy in life, including the creative energy of
the arts. Both this group and the pastoralists are haunted
by the sense of an invisible serenity which has disap-
peared from contemporary life but can be re-experi-
enced through tradition. Often this feeling takes the
form of a sense of vanished gods, like the 'dignified, invisible' presences of Eliot's rose-garden. Yeats tried to
identify these presences with his pantheon of Irish gods
and heroes; Lawrence with his darker gods and his historical myths like that of the Etruscans; George and
other German romantics with the Classical gods; Jung

with unconscious archetypes. Christian writers tend to think more conceptually of the organizing ideas of religion, original sin, Incarnation, a personal power of evil, and the like, as giving a new richness and depth of significance to life, whether of joy or terror. 'I do wish those people who deny the reality of eternal punishment,' said the Catholic poet Lionel Johnson, 'would understand their own dreadful vulgarity.'

One type who most obviously withdraws from the social contract and sets up a way of life in opposition to it is the criminal. There are two kinds of criminals, professional and amateur: those for whom crime is money and those for whom crime is fun. We are concerned with the latter group. It is obvious that the criminal or conspirator is a ready symbol for the artist who breaks with the social contract; one thinks of Joyce's Stephen Dedalus and his conspiratorial motto of silence, exile, and cunning, or Rimbaud's identification of himself as a child of Satan, linked to criminals, slaves, and outcasts of all kinds. The symbol of the artist as criminal, however, goes much deeper. I spoke of the way in which optimistic theories of progress and revolution had grown out of Rousseau's conception of a society of nature and reason buried under the injustices of civilization and awaiting release. But, around the same time, the Marquis de Sade was expounding a very different view of the natural society. According to this, nature teaches us that pleasure is the highest good in life, and the keenest form of pleasure consists in inflicting or suffering pain. Hence the real natural society would not be the reign of equality and reason prophesied by Rousseau: it would be a society in which those who liked tormenting others were set free to do so. So far as evidence is relevant, there is more evidence for de Sade's theory of natural society than there is for Rousseau's. In any case there is an unpleasantly large degree of truth in the sadist vision, and a good many literary conceptions have taken off from it, or near it. One is the cult of the holy sinner, the person who achieves an exceptional awareness, whether religious or aesthetic in character, from acts of cruelty, or, at least, brings about such an awareness in us. Dostoevsky's Stavrogin, Gide's Lafcadio, with his *acte gratuit* or unmotivated crime, the hero of Camus's *L'Etranger* and of Chaplin's *Monsieur Verdoux*, are examples. A good deal of contemporary American writing links not merely picaresque law-breaking, smoking marijuana and the like, but outright violence and terror, with serious social attitudes. There is something of this in Mailer, and a good deal more in LeRoi Jones and other 'black power' adherents. In D. H. Lawrence, too, a curious hysterical cruelty occasionally gets out of hand, most continuously, perhaps, in *The Plumed Serpent*.

Jean Genet is the most remarkable example of the contemporary artist as criminal: his sentence of life imprisonment was appealed against by Sartre, Claudel, Cocteau, and Gide, and even before his best-known works had appeared, Sartre had written a seven-hundred-page biography of him called *Saint Genet*. Genet's most famous play, in this country, is *Le Balcon*. Here the main setting is a brothel in which the patrons dress up as bishops, generals or judges and engage in sadistic ritual games with the whores, who are flogged and abused in the roles of penitents or thieves. The point is that society as a whole is one vast sadistic ritual of this sort. As the mock-bishop says, very rudely, he does not care about the function of bishop: all he wants is the metaphor, the idea or sexual core of the office. The madam of the brothel remarks: 'They all want everything to be as true as possible . . . minus something indefinable, so that it won't be true'—a most accurate description of what I have been calling stupid realism. A revolution is going on outside: it is put down by the chief of police, and the patrons of the brothel are pulled out of it to enact the 'real' social forms of the games they have been playing. Nobody notices the difference, because generals and judges and bishops are traditional metaphors, and new patrons come to the brothel and continue the games. The chief of police, the only one with any real social power, is worried because he is not a traditional metaphor, and nobody comes to the brothel to imitate him. Finally, however, one such patron does turn up: the leader of the revolution. There is a good deal more in the play, but this account will perhaps indicate how penetrating it is as a sadist vision of society.

All these anti-social attitudes in modern culture are, broadly speaking, reactionary. That is, their sense of antagonism to existing society is what is primary, and it is much clearer and more definite than any alternative social ideal. Hugh MacDiarmid, supporting both Communism and Scottish nationalism, and Dos Passos, moving from a simple radicalism to a simple conservatism, are random examples among writers of what sometimes seems a dissent for its own sake. Wherever we turn, we are made aware of the fact that society is a repressive anxiety-structure, and that creative power comes from a part of the mind that resists repression but is not in itself moral or rational. In Vladimir Nabokov's novel, *Pale Fire*, a gentle, wistful, rather touching pastoral poem falls into the hands of a lunatic who proceeds to 'annotate' it with a wild paranoid fantasy about his own adventures as a prince in some European state during a revolution. Poem and commentary have nothing to do with each other, and perhaps that is the only point the book makes. But the title, taken from Shakespeare's *Timon of Athens*, suggests a certain allegory of the relation of art to the wish-fulfilment fantasies that keep bucking and plunging underneath it. Such forces are in all of us, and are strong enough to destroy the world if they are not controlled through release instead of repression. In my last lecture I want to talk about the way in which the creative arts are absorbed into society through education. Meanwhile we may notice that the real basis for the opposition of artist and society is the fact that not merely communications media and public relations, but the whole structure of society itself, is an anti-art, an old and worn-out creation that needs to be created anew.

3

Clair
de lune
intellectuel

THE MODERN WORLD
began with the industrial revolution, and the industrial
revolution set up an economic structure beside the political one which was really a rival form of society. Industry had often enough taken the form of an organization
distinct from the state, but never before in history did
man have so strong a feeling of living under two social
orders as he did in the period of laissez faire. The sepa-
ration could not, of course, last indefinitely, because
the economic social order had so revolutionary an effect
on the political one. Explicitly in Marxism, and more

tentatively in the democracies, all society eventually comes to be thought of as consisting functionally only of workers or producers. Marxism moves in the direction of a final or once-for-all revolution in which the productive society becomes the only society; in the democracies the non-productive groups, or leisure classes, gradually become socially unfunctional. In both types of society, however, there are, in addition to the workers and their directors, a large group who exist to explain, manifest, encourage, rationalize, and promote the various forms of production. In Marxist societies those in this second group are known as party workers; in the democracies, especially in North America, they are thought of as advertisers and educators.

It seems clear that even with the heavy handicap of defence budgets, even with the assistance given to those parts of the world which are committed to the West but are otherwise unfortunate, the productive power of American and other advanced democracies has become so over-efficient that it can continue to function only by various feather-bedding devices. One device, of the type satirized in *Parkinson's Law*, is the subsidizing of employment; another, of the type lamented in *The Feminine Mystique*, is the effort to encourage as many as possible of the female half of the population to devote themselves to becoming full-time consumers. But these devices do not conceal the fact that leisure is growing so rapidly, both in the amount of time and the number of people it affects, as to be a social complex equal in importance to employment itself.

Thus the technological revolution is becoming more and more an educational rather than an industrial phenomenon. For education is the positive aspect of leisure. As long as we think of society, in nineteenth-century terms, as essentially productive, leisure is only spare time, usually filled up with various forms of distraction, and a 'leisure class', which has nothing but spare time, is only a class of parasites. But as soon as we realize that leisure is as genuine and important an aspect of everyone's life as remunerative work, leisure becomes something that also demands discipline and responsibility. Distraction, of the kind one sees on highways and beaches at holiday weekends, is not leisure but a running away from leisure, a refusal to face the test of one's inner resources that spare time poses. It is to genuine leisure what the feather-bedding devices I have just referred to are to genuine industry and business. Our problem today is not that of a leisure class, but of leisure itself, as an increasingly growing factor in the lives of all classes. In relation to the economy, man is essentially functional, deriving his individuality from his job and his social context. In relation to leisure he is essentially a performer or actor, judged, not by his specific role, but by his skill in performance. That is, any leisure activity which is not sheer idleness or distraction depends on some acquired skill, and the acquiring and practice of that skill is a mode of education.

Education involves, first of all, the network of educational institutions: schools and universities, which occupy most of the time and attention of a large part of the population, and many other types of organization—churches, museums, art galleries, theatres, just to start with. To look at our society realistically today, we have to think of its economic or productive aspect as a part of it: let us say, by a rhetorical statistic, half of it. The other half consists of the educational activities which are growing much faster, proportionately, than industry, and which I shall call the leisure structure of society. The industrial and the leisure structures make up, between them, the program of needs and activities which, in their degenerate form in the ancient Roman world, were described as bread and circuses.

In the democracies, as well as in the Communist states, social development has been mainly a matter of relating the economic structure to the political one. In Canada, as in Britain and America, the left wing tends to favour closer relations, usually stopping short of complete socialization, and the right wing tends to favour economic autonomy, usually stopping considerably short of pure laissez faire. Views on the relation of the political to the leisure structure seem to be the reverse of this. Liberal sympathies are more disposed to keep the leisure structure autonomous, and to feel that the political influence on the leisure structure is normally a bad influence. The right wing are more disposed to mutter about the injustice being done to the anti-intellectual majority of taxpayers, and to call for tighter cultural budgets.

In any event the question of what the government does in relation to the leisure structure is taking on an in-

creasingly revolutionary importance. The word 'revolution', which originally suggested conspiracy and barri-
cades in the street, can now, in our society, only be
associated with some kind of centralized action, usually
by the government, in whatever areas can develop
enough freedom of movement to revolutionize anything. At present the so-called mass media are sponsored
mainly by advertising, which means that they are related primarily to the economy: these include television,
newspapers, and the dwindling body of fiction and picture magazines which function as retail advertising
journals. The turning of sponsorship into direct control,
as when an editor is dismissed or a program cancelled for
offending an advertiser, is felt to be pernicious by those
who are not completely cynical in such matters. Every
effort of a government, however timid, to set up national
film and broadcasting companies, and thus to turn over
at least some of the mass media to the leisure structure,
is part of a fateful revolutionary process. So is every
effort to subsidize creative talent; so, even more obviously, is every effort to plan a city more intelligently
than leaving it to speculative blight. We are taking the
first cautious steps on this revolutionary road now, and
it is highly typical of Canada that it is the *administra-
tion* of the leisure structure, questions of dividing responsibility and authority, that should be most eagerly
discussed. The complete control of the leisure structure
by the political or economic power is a logical development of Marxism, at least in its twentieth-century form,
but to us the Marxist attitude to the leisure structure

seems a purely reactionary one. If the growth of the leisure structure is as important and central a development as I think it is, some of the major possibilities of further social development remain with the more industrially advanced democracies.

Schools and universities are mainly for young people, and, under the influence of the view of society as consisting primarily of wage-earners, they have traditionally been thought of as places in which the young are prepared for real life. This view is congenial to the normal tendency of the adult to think of the adolescent as a rudimentary and primitive form of himself. In my own student days during the depression, when so many students came to college because of the difficulty of finding jobs, it was felt that the four years spent in study required some justification. What creates a man's self-respect, it was thought, is the holding of a job as the head of a family, and university appeared merely to postpone this function. Young people in working-class homes felt this even more strongly, and, in my experience, did not much care that most of them were unofficially but effectively excluded from the universities. The greatly increased number attending today reflects of course an increase in both population and economic buoyancy; but when it is said that students go to college because industry and business now require more education, I suspect a hangover of the old self-justifying arguments. I think students come to college because they realize, more clearly than many of their elders, that by doing so they are fully participating in their society, and

can no longer be thought of as getting ready for something else more important.

It inevitably follows from the same principle, however, that the university, or at least the kind of thing
the university does, can hardly remain indefinitely the
exclusive preserve of the young. The question of adult
education is still too large and shapeless for us to be
able to look squarely at it along with all our other
problems of expansion, but, apart from the very large
amount of education within industry itself, the adult
population will also need institutions of teaching and
discussion as the organized form of their leisure time:
I think particularly of married women with grown-up
families. It is difficult for a government not to think
of education in terms of training, and to regard the university as a public-service institution concerned with
training. Such a conception naturally puts a heavy emphasis on youth, who are allegedly being trained for
society, the human resources of the future, as we say.
Adult education will no doubt enter the picture first in
the context of retraining, as it does now in industry,
but before long we shall have to face a growing demand
for an education which has no immediate reference to
training at all.

We have next to consider the relation of the leisure
structure to the arts. Down to the nineteenth century,
painters, poets, composers tended to follow the traditions set by their predecessors, imitating them and carry-
ing on their conventions in a more elaborate way. Thus
there was a steady increase in self-awareness and com-

93

plexity, and a process resembling that of aging, with each generation building on what had been done up to that point. With the nineteenth century there came, along with the continuing of this process, a prodigious lateral expansion in influence. It was mainly in the second half of the nineteenth century that the great museums came into being, at least in their present form, and the museums brought together an immense assemblage, not merely of works of art, but of objects that presented analogies to and suggestions for the arts. The result was to provide the artist with an encyclopaedic range of influences; it made the artist an academician instead of an apprentice learning from masters. What the museums did for the visual arts modern recordings have done for music.

The increase of historical knowledge, of which archaeology formed a central part, was so vast as to make it seem as though the cemeteries were on the march, the entire past awakening to an aesthetic apocalypse. Painters and sculptors in particular were presented with a world-wide panorama of creative skills, very largely in the applied or so-called 'minor' arts. This was naturally an important influence on the trend to formalism that I spoke of in my last lecture, for what this panorama revealed was primarily a universal language of design. Design in its turn has provided a basis for the unifying of the 'major' and 'minor' arts. Anyone today comparing an exhibition of modern painting or sculpture with one of textiles or pottery gets the impression that in the modern period there is really only an art of design, which is applied equally to all the visual arts, major and minor. I have referred to the view of William Morris, at the threshold of the modern period, that the minor or useful arts were a key area in social revolution because they represent, more clearly than the major arts, the imagination as a way of life, as providing the visible forms of a free society. Although social developments have not followed Morris's anti-mechanistic anarchism, it is still no doubt true that the principles which link such a painter as Mondriaan to textile or ceramic design are a part of a considerable democratizing of aesthetic experience. If so, Morris was right in seeing a significant social, even a political dimension in modern cultural developments.

Along with archaeology and its 'museum without walls', as it has been called, came anthropology and its study of 'primitive' cultures, which brought primitive art, with its weird stylizing of form, its openly phallic and sexual themes, its deliberate distortion of perspective, squarely in front of the artist's eye. Of all elements in the modern tradition, perhaps that of primitive art, of whatever age or continent, has had the most pervasive influence. The primitive, with its immediate connexion with magic, expresses a directness of imaginative impact which is naive and yet conventionalized, spontaneous and yet precise. It indicates most clearly the way in which a long and tired tradition of Western art, which has been refining and sophisticating itself for centuries, can be revived, or even reborn. Perhaps the kinship between the primitive and ourselves goes even deeper: it has frequently been remarked that we may be, if we survive, the primitives of an unknown culture, the cave men of a new mental era.

It is not always realized how closely analogous the developments of modern literature are to those in the visual arts. The world-wide panorama of the museums is not attainable in literature with the same immediacy, because of the barriers of language. Linguistics sometimes gives an illusion of having surmounted these barriers, but the illusion of literature in translation is even less convincing. However, the trend to formalism, stylizing, and abstraction is quite as marked in poetry as in painting. The elements of verbal design are myth and metaphor, both of which are modes of identification. That is, they are primitive and naïve associations of things, a sun and a god, a hero and a lion, which turn their backs on realism or accurate descriptive statement. In literature, as in painting, realism was an emancipating force down to the nineteenth century, when it reached its culmination in the great novelists of that period. The modern period begins with Baudelaire and the *symbolisme* that followed him, and literature ever since has been increasingly organized by symbolism, dense and often difficult metaphor, myth, especially in drama, and folktale. This development was anticipated in the great mythopoeic poetry of the Romantics, especially Blake, Shelley, and Keats, who correspond in poetry to the revolution of Turner in painting. Like the parallel developments in visual art, the increase of consciously employed myth and metaphor is also an increase in erudition and the conscious awareness of tradition.

When the Romantic movement began, there was one important primitive influence on it, that of the oral ballads, which began to be collected and classified at that time. The oral ballad makes a functional use of refrains and other strongly marked patterns of repetition, which correspond to the emphasis on design in the primitive pictorial arts. The fact that it depended for survival on an oral tradition meant that whatever personal turns of phrase there may originally have been in it were smoothed out, the poem thus acquiring a kind of stripped poetic surface quite unlike that of written poetry. The literary ballads which imitate these characteristics—the *Lyrical Ballads* of Wordsworth and Coleridge, Blake's *Mental Traveller*, Keats's *La Belle Dame Sans Merci*—come about as close as poetry can come to reproducing directly the voice of the creative powers of the mind below consciousness, a voice which is uninhibited and yet curiously impersonal as well. This was also the 'democratic' voice that Whitman attempted to reproduce, and Whitman is the godfather of all the folk singing and other oral developments of our time which cover so large an area of contemporary popular culture. A different but related Canadian tradition is that of the *chansonniers*, as represented today by Gilles Vigneault.

Fifty years ago it could be said that the university and the creative artist were at opposite ends of the cultural spectrum. The university, on its humanistic side, ran a critical and scholarly establishment concerned with the past, and related itself to the present by translating the values of the past into contemporary middle-class values. Anyone interested in painting or writing was likely to drop out of school as soon as it had wasted the legal amount of his time and devote himself to living precariously by his wits. I spent a dinner talking to such a (Canadian) writer recently: he told me of how he had left school at grade ten and eventually established himself as a writer, of how his life since had been financially difficult, even despairing at times, but redeemed by the excitement of an unexpected sale, or, more genuinely, by occasional gleams of satisfaction over a creative job well done. A century ago this would have been a familiar type of story, but while I listened with interest and respect, because I knew his work and admired it, I felt that I was hearing one of the last legends of a vanishing species, of a way of life that was going and would not return.

For in the last few decades the leisure structure has become much more integrated. The university's interest in contemporary culture is now practically obsessive, nor is its relation to it confined to mere interest. More and more of the established artists are on its teaching staff, and more and more of the younger rebels are their undergraduate students. While serving on a committee for awarding fellowships to Canadian writers, I noticed that practically all the serious English candidates were employed by universities and practically all the French ones by the National Film Board or the Canadian Broadcasting Corporation. What cultural differences this implied I do not know, but for both groups some professional connexion with the leisure structure was so regular as to amount practically to a closed shop. When the beatnik movement began about ten years ago, it seemed as though an anti-academic, even anti-intellectual tendency was consolidating around a new kind of cultural experience. It attracted certain types of expression, such as the improvising swing ensembles and their derivatives, which had traditionally been well outside the orbit of higher education. But the academics got interested in them too, and vice versa.

The nineteenth-century artist was typically a loner: even in the twentieth he was often the last stand of laissez faire, resisting every kind of social mediation between himself and his public. It is still often asserted that he ought to continue to be so, and should avoid the seductions of university posts and foundation grants. The social facts of yesterday are the clichés of today. But he is now in a world where such agencies as the Canada Council represent a growing concern on the part of society with the leisure structure. This has affected all aspects of the arts: we may note particularly the changes in genre. Some arts, like music and drama, are ensemble performances for audience; others, like the novel and the easel-painting, are individualized. In an intensely individualized era like the Victorian age, the novel goes up and the drama goes down. Up until quite recently, the creative person, say in literature, was typically one who 'wanted to write', and what he wanted

99

to write was usually poetry or fiction. He might dream of rivalling Shakespeare, but he would be unlikely to want Shakespeare's job of a busy actor-manager in a profit-sharing corporation. It looks as though creative interests were shifting again to the dramatic: it is Pinter and Albee and Beckett on the stage, Bergman and Fellini and others in film, who seem to be making cultural history today, as the novelists were making it a century ago. The creative undergraduate tends less to bring his sheaf of poems to his instructor, and tends more to ask his advice about where he can get financial assistance, private or foundational, as a result of having gone broke with a film-making or dramatic venture. This may be a temporary vogue, but I think not, and of course it is obvious how this kind of creative interest immediately involves the artist in the social aspects of the leisure structure. (Psychotherapy, so profoundly connected with the contemporary imagination, has recently changed its emphasis from narrative and confessional techniques to dramatic ones, which is perhaps another aspect of the same cultural trend.)

In my earlier talks I spoke of the modern imagination as resisting the pressure of advertising and propaganda, which assume and try to bring about a passive response. Advertising and propaganda come respectively from the economic and the political structures, and I touched on the neurosis in modern life which springs from the feeling that these structures are not worth loyalty. For all our dislike of the word totalitarian, we have to recognize that there is a profound and genuine, if ultimately specious, appeal in any form of social activity which promises to expand into a complete way of life, engaging all aspects of one's interests and providing fulfilment for one's cultural, spiritual, and intellectual as well as social needs. A generation ago many people plunged into radical politics in the hope of finding a total program of this kind, but all forms of politics, including the radical form, seem sooner or later to dwindle into a specialized chess game. Many others at various times have sought the same total activity in religion, a more promising place, but often a disappointing one, with rather second-rate cultural rewards. It would simplify my argument considerably at this point if I could say that the leisure structure was the missing piece of society, that it is what we can give an unqualified loyalty to, and that it does fulfil the entire range of non-material human needs. There is however no reason to suppose that the leisure structure, as it grows in social importance, will produce a social institution any better (if no worse) than business or politics do: the most we can hope for is a system of checks and balances which will prevent any one of our new three estates from becoming too powerful. Even Plato hardly went so far as to believe in the perfectibility of intellectuals, and the history of the Christian Church, which started out with a much higher ideal of loyalty, does not encourage us to feel that any social institution can be a genuine embodiment of a social ideal. It is mainly those in the departments concerned with the arts, humanities, and general education who show a clear difference of social attitude, not because their virtue is superior, but because their budgets are low. The rich grants that scientists and administrators can obtain as employees of government and industry will always be attractive, whatever their relation to academic freedom, a relation which in itself will become much hazier as universities become more dependent financially on government.

I should describe the ideal or Utopian features of the leisure structure, along with the political and economic ones, rather differently. The evolution of political democracy, as it fought against entrenched privilege at first, and then against dictatorial tendencies, has to some extent been a genuine evolution of an idea of liberty, however often betrayed and perverted, and however much threatened still. The evolution of industry into a society of producers, as labour continued to fight against a managerial oligarchy, has been to a correspondingly modified extent an evolution of an idea of equality. Matthew Arnold warned the dominant bourgeoisie of Victorian England that a society could pursue liberty to the point of forgetting about equality. Today, with capitalism in a counter-reformation period and with totalitarianism thought of as something foreign, we prefer to be reminded that society—that is, other societies—can pursue equality to the point of forgetting about liberty. But neither political democracy nor trade unions have developed much sense of the third revolutionary ideal of fraternity—the word 'comrade' has for most of us a rather sinister and frigid sound. Fraternity is perhaps the ideal that the leisure structure has to contribute to society. A society of students, scholars, and artists is a society of neighbours, in the genuinely religious sense of that word. That is, our neighbour is not, or not necessarily, the person in the same national or ethnical or class group with ourselves, but may be a 'good Samaritan' or person to whom we are linked by deeper bonds than nationality or racism or class solidarity can any longer provide. These are bonds of intellect and imagination as well as of love and good will. The neighbour of a scientist is another scientist working on similar lines, perhaps in a different continent; the neighbour of a novelist writing about Mississippi is (as Faulkner indicated in his Nobel Prize speech) anybody anywhere who can respond to his work. The fact that feuds among scholars and artists are about as bitter as feuds ever get will doubtless make for some distinction between theory and practice.

It is a peculiarity of North America today that culture is absorbed into society mainly through the university classroom. Such a dependence of contemporary culture on the educational system, rather than on a self-acquired social education supplementing the academic one, is much less true of Europe. This seems to imply, perhaps correctly, a higher degree of maturity in European society, in this respect at least. When I speak of the North American university's interest in contemporary culture as obsessive I am speaking of a degree of interest that I somewhat regret: it might be better if the university confined itself to supplying the historical dimension of its culture. But the students dictate a great deal of the teaching program of the university, though they seldom realize it, and students of the humanities appear to regard the study of the contemporary or near-contemporary as the most liberalizing element of a liberal education. My notion is that the trend is for the European pattern to fall in with the North American one rather than the other way round, but my observations do not depend on such a prediction.

Whatever the eventual relation of teaching and culture, the academic and the creative aspects of contemporary society have certainly come together within the last generation or so, and their future destinies, so far as one can see into the future, appear to be closely linked. This accounts for a feature of our cultural life which seems more paradoxical than it is. The university classroom is concerned with 'liberal' education, and liberal education is liberal in every sense of the word: it emancipates, it is tolerant, it assimilates the learning process to a social idea. Yet so far as it is concerned with contemporary culture, its material includes all the reactionary and anti-social attitudes I glanced at earlier, some of which are, in detail, quite obviously silly, perverse, or wrong-headed. But when contemporary authors are assigned for compulsory reading, and when they are taught in a way that relates them to their cultural heritage, a certain detachment comes into the attitude toward them. Not all the detachment is good, but one thing about it is: the social attitude of the writer is taken over by the social attitude of education itself, and loses its crankiness by being placed in a social context. Study, as distinct from direct response, is a cool medium, and even the most blatant advocacy of violence and terror may be, like Satan in the Bible, transformed into an angel of light by being regarded as a contribution to modern thought. Where shall wisdom be found? Chiefly, for our age, in the imaginative and technical skills of the more or less unwise.

The leisure structure, then, is essentially a structure of education, which means that it is vitally concerned with teaching. One can teach only what is teachable, and what the university must teach is the only thing it can teach: the specific disciplines into which genuine knowledge is divided. What results from this in the mind of the student? Facts, perhaps; ideas; information; the techniques of the present; the traditions of the past. But all these things are quickly acquired by the good student, and, unless used for some definite purpose, quickly forgotten. What emerges from university teaching, as its final result in the student's mind, is something the university cannot, or should not, explicitly teach. As most great theorists of education, from Castiglione to Newman, have recognized, the form of liberal education is social, in the broadest sense, rather than simply intellectual. I should call the social form of liberal education, provisionally, a vision of society, or, more technically, a mythology.

In every age there is a structure of ideas, images, beliefs, assumptions, anxieties, and hopes which express the view of man's situation and destiny generally held at that time. I call this structure a mythology, and its units myths. A myth, in this sense, is an expression of man's concern about himself, about his place in the scheme of things, about his relation to society and God, about the ultimate origin and ultimate fate, either of himself or of the human species generally. A mythology is thus a product of human concern, of our involvement with ourselves, and it always looks at the world from a man-centred point of view. The early and primitive myths were stories, mainly stories about gods, and their units were physical images. In more highly structured societies they develop in two different but related directions. In the first place, they develop into literature as we know it, first into folktales and legends of heroes, thence into the conventional plots of fiction and metaphors of poetry. In the second place, they become conceptualized, and become the informing principles of historical and philosophical thought, as the myth of fall becomes the informing idea of Gibbon's history of Rome, or the myth of the sleeping beauty Rousseau's buried society of nature and reason. My first lecture dealt primarily with mythology in this sense, particularly with the so-called existential myths.

It seems to me that there have been two primary mythological constructions in Western culture. One was the vast synthesis that institutional Christianity made of its Biblical and Aristotelian sources. This myth is at its clearest in the Middle Ages, but it persisted for centuries later, and much of its structure, though greatly weakened by the advance of science, was still standing in the eighteenth century itself. The other is the modern mythology that began when the modern world did, in the later eighteenth century, but reached its more specifically modern shape a century later, and a century before now.

The older mythology was one that stressed two things in particular: the subject-object relation and the use of reason. Man was a subject confronting a nature set over against him. Both man and nature were creatures of God, and were united by that fact. There were no gods in nature: if man looked into the powers of nature to find such gods they would soon turn into devils. What he should look at nature for is the evidence of purpose and design which it shows as a complementary creation of God, and the reason can grasp this sense of design. The rational approach to nature was thus superior to the empirical and experimental approach to it, and the sciences that were most deductive and closest to mathematics were those that were first developed. Of all sciences, astronomy is the most dependent on the subject-object relationship, and in the Middle Ages particularly, astronomy was the science par excellence, the one science that a learned medieval poet, such as Dante or Chaucer, would be assumed to know.

In the pre-modern myth man's ultimate origin was of God, and his chief end was to draw closer to God. Even more important, the social discipline which raised him above the rest of creation was a divine ordinance. Law was of God; the forms of human civilization, the city and the garden, were imitations of divine models, for God planted the garden of Eden and had established his city before man was created; the ultimate human community was not in this world, but in a heaven closer to the divine presence. Philosophers recognized that the ordinary categories of the mind, such as our perception of time and space, might not be adequate at a purely spiritual level. It was possible, for example, that a spiritual body, such as an angel, did not occupy space or travel in space at all. The unfortunate wretch who attempted to put this question into a lively and memorable form by asking how many angels could stand on the point of a pin has become a byword for pedantic stupidity, a terrible warning to all instructors who try to make a technical subject interesting. But as far as popular belief and poetic imagery were concerned, the spiritual world was thought of as essentially another objective environment, to be described in symbols— city, temple, garden, streets—derived from human life, though the myth taught that human life had been derived from them. This mythology, relating as it did both man and nature to God, was a total one, so complete and far-reaching that an alternative world-picture was practically unthinkable. This is the real significance of Voltaire's familiar epigram, that if God did not exist it would be necessary to invent him, which was, in his day, a much more serious remark than it sounds. One could, theoretically, be an atheist; but even an atheist would find God blocking his way on all sides: he would meet the hypothesis of God in history, in philosophy, in psychology, in astronomy. As for morality, its standards were so completely assimilated to religious sanctions that even a century ago it was impossible for many people to believe that non-religious man could have any moral integrity at all.

In the eighteenth century there began to grow, slowly but irresistibly, the conviction that man had created his own civilization. This meant not merely that he was responsible for it—he had always been that—but that its forms of city and garden and design, of law and social discipline and education, even, ultimately, of morals and religion, were of human origin and human creation. This new feeling crystallized around Rousseau in the eighteenth century, and the assumptions underlying the American and French revolutions were relatively new assumptions. Liberty was no longer, as it had been for Milton, something that God gives and that man resists: it was something that most men want and that those who have a stake in slavery invoke their gods to prevent them from getting. Law was no longer, as it had been for Hooker, the reflection of divine order in human life, but in large part the reflection of class privilege in property rights. Art and culture were no longer, as they had been for the age of Shakespeare, the ornaments of social discipline: they took on a prophetic importance as portraying the forms of civilization that man had created. The Romantic movement brought in the conception of the 'serious' artist, setting his face against society to follow his art, from which the modern antagonism of the artist to society that I discussed earlier has descended.

A major principle of the older mythology was the

correspondence of human reason with the design and purpose in nature which it perceives. This correspondence was still accepted even after God had dwindled into a deistic first cause, a necessary hypothesis and nothing more. The modern movement, properly speaking, began when Darwin finally shattered the old teleological conception of nature as reflecting an intelligent purpose. From then on design in nature has been increasingly interpreted by science as a product of a self-developing nature. The older view of design survives vestigially, as when religion tells us that some acts are 'contrary to nature'. But contemporary science, which is professionally concerned with nature, does not see in the ancient mother-goddess the Wisdom which was the bride of a superhuman creator. What it sees rather is a confused old beldame who has got where she has through a remarkable obstinacy in adhering to trial and error—mostly error—procedures. The rational design that nature reflects is in the human mind only. An example of the kind of thinking that Darwin has made impossible for the modern mind is: 'If the Lord had intended us to fly, he'd have given us wings.' The conception of natural functions as related to a personal and creative intention is no longer in our purview.

Modern mythology, at least with us, is naturally not as well unified as the earlier one, but it does possess some unity none the less. It reaches us on two main levels. There is a social mythology, which we learn through conversation and the contacts of family, teachers, and neighbours, which is reinforced by the mass media, newspapers, television, and movies, and which is based fundamentally on cliché and stock response. In the United States, elementary education, at least before the sputnik revolution of 1957, consisted very largely of acquiring a stock-response mythology known as the American way of life. Canadian elementary teaching has been less obsessed by social mythology, as its children do not require the indoctrination that citizens of a great world power do, but it has its own kind, as in fact do all societies in all ages. Social mythology in our day is a faint parody of the Christian mythology which preceded it. 'Things were simpler in the old days; the world has unaccountably lost its innocence since we were children. I just live to get out of this rat race for a bit and go somewhere where I can get away from it all. Yet there is a bracing atmosphere in competition and we may hope to see consumer goods enjoyed by all members of our society after we abolish poverty. The world is threatened with grave dangers from foreigners, perhaps with total destruction; yet if we dedicate ourselves anew to the tasks which lie before us we may preserve our way of life for generations yet unborn.' One recognizes the familiar outlines of paradise myths, fall myths, exodus-from-Egypt myths, pastoral myths, apocalypse myths.

The first great modern novelist is usually taken to be Flaubert, whose last and unfinished work, *Bouvard et Pécuchet*, included, as part of its scheme, a 'Dictionary of Accepted Ideas'. In recent years there has been a phenomenal growth of books which are written from within one of the social sciences, but are actually read as social satires. Anyone can think of a dozen titles: *The Lonely Crowd, The Affluent Society, The Organization Man, The Academic Market-Place, The Status Seekers, The Insolent Chariots, The Hidden Persuaders, Games People Play.* This last one breaks the rhythm of the conventional titles: a stock phrase preceded by the inside-knowledge suggestion of the definite article. Not all of these are good books, but they all deal with subjects about which good books ought to be written. The importance of this form of literary fiction, for that is what it is, is that it studies society from the point of view of its popular or cliché mythology, its accepted ideas. It is bound to have a revolutionary impact on other fiction by making novelists and dramatists more aware of the symbolic and ritual basis of social behaviour.

A more complicated mythology emerges in general education and liberal arts courses, where we become aware of the immense importance of the thinkers who have helped to shape our mythology: Rousseau, Marx, Freud, the existentialists, and others whose importance depends on what versions of it we take most seriously. In addition to the art and scholarship which is specialized and works with limited objectives, there is a wide variety of 'idea books', books that survey the intellectual world, or a large section of it, from a certain comprehensive point of view. On the bookshelves of my study in front of me as I write I see works of history: Spengler's *Decline of the West*, Toynbee's *A Study of*

History, Hannah Arendt's *Origins of Totalitarianism*. Works of philosophy: Whitehead's *Science and the Modern World*, Sartre's *Being and Nothing*. Works of science: Eddington's *Nature of the Physical World*, Sherrington's *Man on his Nature*. Works of criticism: McLuhan's *Understanding Media*, Fiedler's *An End to Innocence*, Harold Rosenberg's *The Tradition of the New*, Irving Howe's *Steady Work*. Works of psychology: Norman Brown's *Life Against Death*, Marcuse's *Eros and Civilization*. Works of religion: Buber's *I and Thou*, Tillich's *The Courage to Be*, Cox's *The Secular City*. This is a purely random list, but it should give an idea of the kind of book that helps to shape our contemporary mythology, and to give coherence and co-ordination to our views of the human situation. All these books deal with ideas, but occasional words in the titles, 'Decline', 'City', 'Eros', 'Innocence', indicate their origin in myth. In a sense they are all philosophical, even though most of them are clearly something other than actual philosophy. What I am here calling mythology has in fact often been regarded as the rightful function of philosophy, and we note that philosophers, especially of the existentialist school, have been particularly fertile in naming our central myths, such as the alienation, absurdity, anxiety, and nausea dealt with in my first lecture.

Our mythology, I said, is a structure built by human concern: it is existential in the broad sense, and deals with the human situation in terms of human hopes and fears. Thus, though some of the books I have listed are written from the point of view of a scientific discipline, it does not really include the physical sciences. In our day, ever since Darwin, there have been two world-pictures: the picture of the world we see, which is simply there, and is not man-centred, and the picture of the world we make, which is necessarily man-centred. The arts, the humanities, and in part the social sciences, all contribute to the contemporary myth of concern, but the physical sciences have their own structure, perhaps their own mythology. The earlier mythology was developed out of the idea of God; God has today no status, even as a hypothesis, in physical science, but the myth of concern neither excludes nor necessitates God, who comes into some versions of it and not into others. Of course scientific conceptions are continually being annexed by mythographers: the conception of evolution, for instance, has been applied in dozens of ways. But when the term evolution is used in Bernard Shaw's theory of a divine creative will, in Herbert Spencer's philosophy of ethics, in a Biblical scholar's account of the growth of the idea of God, or in a history of painting, the conception used is not identical with the biological theory: it is only a mythological analogy of that theory. How significant the analogy is has still to be determined, as a separate problem. Naturally science has immense relevance to the myth of concern, especially when it manifests an ability to destroy or to improve human existence—in some areas, such as genetics, it is not always easy to distinguish the two things. But it is a primary function of the myth of concern to judge the effects of science on human life in its own terms. This is what good mythological works written by scientists, such as the books of Eddington and Jeans and Sherrington, help us to do. When a mythologist attempts to show that the conceptions of science support or prove his vision, he weakens his power of resistance to science.

What I am describing is a liberal or 'open' mythology, of the sort appropriate to a democracy. I call it a structure, but it is often so fluid that the solid metaphor of structure hardly applies to it at all. Each man has his own version of it, conditioned by what he knows best, and in fact he will probably adopt several differing versions in the course of his life. Myths are seldom if ever actual hypotheses that can be verified or refuted; that is not their function: they are co-ordinating or integrating ideas. Hence, though good mythological books are usually written by competent scholars, the mythology of concern is something different from actual scholarship, and is subordinate to it. Any verified fact or definitely refuted theory may alter the whole mythological structure at any time, and must be allowed to do so. Yet there are certain assumptions which give mythology some social unity and make discussion, argument, and communication possible. It is not addressed directly to belief: it is rather a reservoir of possibilities of belief. It is the area of free discussion which Mill, in his *Essay on Liberty*, felt to be the genuine parliament of man and the safeguard of social freedom as a whole. It is the 'culture' that Matthew Arnold opposed to the anarchy of doing as one likes, the check on social and political activism. For activism, however well motivated, is always based on rationalized stock response. Beliefs and convictions and courses of action come out of an open mythology, but when such courses are decided on, the area of discussion is not closed off. No idea is anything more than a half-truth unless it contains its own opposite, and is expanded by its own denial or qualification.

An open mythology of this kind is very different from a closed one, which is a structure of belief. There are two aspects of belief, theoretical and practical. Theoretical belief is a creed, a statement of what a man says he believes, thinks he believes, believes he believes. A creed is essentially an assertion that one belongs to a certain social body: even if one is trying to define an individual belief not exactly like anyone else's, one is still defining one's social and intellectual context. One's profession of faith is a part of one's social contract. Practical belief is what a man's actions and attitudes show that he believes. Pascal's conception of the 'wager', the assumptions underlying one's conduct, is a conception of practical belief. Similar conceptions are in Newman's *Grammar of Assent*, and, more generally, in Vaihinger's theory of assumed fictions. A closed mythology, like Christianity in the Middle Ages, requires the statement of theoretical belief from everyone, and imposes a discipline that will make practice consistent with it. Thus the closed mythology is a statement both of what is believed to be true and of what is going to be made true by a certain course of action. This latter more particularly is the sense in which Marxism is a closed mythology, and the sense in which another revolutionary thinker, Sorel, generally conceives of myth.

A closed mythology forms a body of major premises which is superior in authority to scholarship and art. A closed myth already contains all the answers, at least potentially: whatever scholarship or art produce has to be treated deductively, as reconcilable with the mythology, or, if irreconcilable, suppressed. In Marxist countries the physical sciences are allowed to function more or less independently of the myth, because, as remarked earlier, society picks up too many of its golden eggs to want to kill the goose, but as the physical sciences do not form an integral part of the myth of concern, their autonomy, up to a point, would not be fatal to it. A closed myth creates a general élite. In the Middle Ages this élite consisted of clerics; in Marxist countries it consists of those who understand both the principles of Marxism and the way that the existing power structure wants Marxism rationalized.

In the democracies there are many who would like to see a closed myth take over. Some are hysterical, like the John Birch society who want a myth of the American way of life, as they understand it, imposed on everything, or like the maudlin Teutonism which a generation ago welcomed the formulating of the Nazi closed myth in Alfred Rosenberg's *Myth of the Twentieth Century*. It may be significant that the book which actually bears that title should be one of the most foolish and mischievous books of our time. Some are nostalgic intellectuals, usually with a strong religious bias, who are bemused by the 'unity' of medieval culture and would like to see some kind of 'return' to it. Some are people who can readily imagine themselves as belonging to the kind of élite that a closed myth would produce. Some are sincere believers in democracy who feel that democracy is at a disadvantage in not having a clear and unquestioned program of its beliefs. But democracy can hardly function with a closed myth, and books of the type I have mentioned as contributions to our mythology, however illuminating and helpful, cannot, in a free society, be given any authority beyond what they earn by their own merits. That is, an open mythology has no canon. Similarly, there can be no general élite in a democratic society: in a democracy everybody belongs to some kind of élite, which derives from its social function a particular knowledge or skill that no other group has.

The earlier closed mythology of the Western world was a religion, and the emergence of an open mythology has brought about a cultural crisis which is at bottom a religious crisis. Traditionally, there are two elements in religion, considered as such apart from a definite faith. One is the primitive element of *religio*, the collection of duties, rituals, and observances which are binding on all members of a community. In this sense Marxism and the American way of life are religions. The other is the sense of a transcendence of the ordinary categories of human experience, a transcendence normally expressed by the words infinite and eternal. As a structure of belief, religion is greatly weakened; it has

no secular power to back it up, and its mandates affect far fewer people, and those far less completely, than a century ago. What is significant is not so much the losing of faith as the losing of guilt feelings about losing it. Religion tends increasingly to make its primary impact, not as a system of taught and learned belief, but as an imaginative structure which, whether 'true' or not, has imaginative consistency and imaginative informing power. In other words, it makes its essential appeal as myth or possible truth, and whatever belief it attracts follows from that.

This means that the arts, which address the imagination, have, ever since the Romantic movement, acquired increasingly the role of the agents through which religion is understood and appreciated. The arts have taken on a prophetic function in society, never more of one than when the artist pretends to deprecate such a role, as, for instance, T. S. Eliot did. It is sometimes said that the arts, especially poetry, have become a 'substitute' for religion, but this makes no sense. The arts contain no objects of worship or belief, nor do they constitute (except professionally for a few people) a way of life. If a man is brought up to believe, say, in the immortality of the soul, loses that belief, and then reconciles himself to death by saying that he will continue to live in the memories of his friends, he really does have a substitute for religion—that is, an accommodation of a transcendent religious conception to the categories of ordinary experience. Many 'philosophies of life', like that of Sartre in our day, are substitutes for religion in this sense, but the arts are not and never can be. The alliance of religion and art is based on the fact that religion deals with transcendent conceptions and that the arts, being imaginative, are confined, not by the limits of the possible, but by the limits of the conceivable. Thus poetry speaks the mythical language of religion. And perhaps, if we think of the reality of religion as mythical rather than doctrinal, religion would turn out to be what is really open about an open mythology: the sense that there are no limits to what the human imagination may conceive or be concerned with.

I developed my own view of such questions by studying the poetry of William Blake. Most of Blake's lyrical poems are either songs of innocence or songs of experience. One of the songs of innocence is a poem called 'The Lamb', where a child asks a lamb the first question of the catechism, 'who made you?' The child has a confident answer: Christ made the lamb because he is both a lamb and child himself, and unites the human and subhuman worlds in a divine personality. The contrasting poem is the song of experience called 'The Tyger', where the poet asks: 'Did he who made the lamb make thee?' Some students of Blake, I regret to say, have tried to answer the question. The vision of the world as created by a benevolent and intelligent power is the innocent vision, the vision of the child who assumes that the world around him must have parents too. Further, it is a world in which only lambs can live: lions and tigers can enter it only on condition that they lie down with the lamb, and thereby cease to be lions and tigers.

But the child's vision is far behind us. The world we are in is the world of the tiger, and that world was never created or seen to be good. It is the subhuman world of nature, a world of law and of power but not of intelligence or design. Things 'evolve' in it, whatever that means, but there is no creative power in it that we can see except that of man himself. And man is not very good at the creating business: he is much better at destroying, for most of him, like an iceberg, is submerged in a destructive element.

Hence the fragility of all human creations and ideals, including the ideal that we are paying tribute to this year. The world we see and live in, and most of the world we have made, belongs to the alienated and absurd world of the tiger. But in all our efforts to imagine or realize a better society, some shadow falls across it of the child's innocent vision of the impossible created world that makes human sense. If we can no longer feel that this world was once created for us by a divine parent, we still must feel, more intensely than ever, that it is the world we ought to be creating, and that whatever may be divine in our destiny or nature is connected with its creation. The loss of faith in such a world is centrally a religious problem, but it has a political dimension as well, and one which includes the question we have been revolving around all through: what is it, in society, to which we really owe loyalty? The question is not easy to answer in Canada. We are alienated from our economy in Marx's sense, as we own relatively little of it ourselves; our governments are democratic: that is, they are what Nietzsche calls 'all too human'. We have few ready-made symbols of loyalty: a flag perfunctorily designed by a committee, a national anthem with its patent pending, an imported Queen. But we may be looking in the wrong direction.

I referred earlier to Grove's *A Search for America*, where the narrator keeps looking for the genuine America buried underneath the America of hustling capitalism which occupies the same place. This buried America is an ideal that emerges in Thoreau, Whitman, and the personality of Lincoln. All nations have such a buried or uncreated ideal, the lost world of the lamb and the child, and no nation has been more preoccupied with it than Canada. The painting of Tom Thomson and Emily Carr, and later of Riopelle and Borduas, is an exploring, probing painting, tearing apart the physical world to see what lies beyond or through it. Canadian literature even at its most articulate, in the poetry of Pratt, with its sense of the corruption at the heart of achievement, or of Nelligan with its sense of unfulfilled clarity, a reach exceeding the grasp, or in the puzzled and indignant novels of Grove, seems constantly to be trying to understand something that eludes it, frustrated by a sense that there is something to be found that has not been found, something to be heard that the world is too noisy to let us hear. One of the derivations proposed for the word Canada is a Portuguese phrase meaning 'nobody here'. The etymology of the word Utopia is very similar, and perhaps the real Canada is an ideal with nobody in it. The Canada to which we really do

owe loyalty is the Canada that we have failed to create. In a year bound to be full of discussions of our identity, I should like to suggest that our identity, like the real identity of all nations, is the one that we have failed to achieve. It is expressed in our culture, but not attained in our life, just as Blake's new Jerusalem to be built in England's green and pleasant land is no less a genuine ideal for not having been built there. What there is left of the Canadian nation may well be destroyed by the kind of sectarian bickering which is so much more interesting to many people than genuine human life. But, as we enter a second century contemplating a world where power and success express themselves so much in stentorian lying, hypnotized leadership, and panic-stricken suppression of freedom and criticism, the un-created identity of Canada may be after all not so bad a heritage to take with us.

The cultural development of Canada

An address delivered to the Social Sciences and Humanities Research Council of Canada and associated scholars at Hart House, University of Toronto, 17 October 1990.

CANADA HAS HAD a far less bloody and violent history than most countries, but Canadians have lived through as much history as any other nation, and the pattern of that history is closely related to events everywhere else in the world. The pivot around which our history turns is, of course, the confederation of 1867, which was a romantic and imperialistic idea, consolidating into a nation a group of British-controlled colonies and territories. In many respects it was by no means an ignoble idea, and the documents leading up to it, such as the Quebec Act and the Durham Report, were, by the standards of their time, based on sane and balanced conceptions.

The main thing wrong with Confederation was its impoverished cultural basis. It was thought of, however unconsciously, as a British colony and a Tory counterpart of the United States, with French and indigenous groups forming picturesque variations in the background. Treaties were made with the indigenous people, but as it was widely assumed that they would soon become extinct or assimilated it made little difference what the treaties said. Students of my generation were taught in school to sing 'The Maple Leaf Forever', which almost attained the status of a national anthem in English Canada, though its attitude to British imperialism sounds pathetic enough in 1990.

There are, as I see it, three aspects of the word culture. First, there is culture as a life-style, shown by the way a society eats, drinks, clothes itself, and carries on its normal social rituals. The British pub and the French bistro represent a cultural difference in life-style of this sort. Second, there is culture as a shared heritage of historical memories and customs, carried out mainly through a common language. Third, there is culture in the shape of what is genuinely created in a society: its literature, music, architecture, science, scholarship, and applied arts. In the years following Confederation, Canada could hardly be said to have had a culture in any of these areas. There was no distinctively Canadian life-style, there was some sense of a common tradition in French Canada, but not much elsewhere; the arts and sciences were minor and provincial. On the Mercator maps usually studied in school, Canada was a huge land mass extending to the ends of the earth, full of rivers, lakes and islands that few Canadians had ever seen; the inhabited part of the country looked only like what the United States had left, a country longer and more divided than Chile. To make a nation out of the stops on the Intercolonial and Canadian Pacific lines seemed as chimerical a notion as building an African civilization on a Cape-to-Cairo railway.

In the eighteenth century the French lost Canada largely because they had no interest in holding it: they sold Louisiana to the United States a few years later, and that probably indicates what the fate of a French Canada would have been. With no social structure left of its own, French Canada fell under the control of the Catholic Church, which was profoundly alienated by the atheistic and anti-clerical French Revolution. As for the British, once they succeeded in occupying Canada their interest in it remained lukewarm, and Canadians in England constantly felt that they would have been regarded with more respect if they had belonged to an independent nation like the United States. The pioneering literature of the nineteenth century continually conveys the feeling that Canada was a kind of non-criminal penal colony, designed for remittance men and Irish housemaids. The Americans made two attempts to occupy the country by military force, both of them beaten off, but violence and the threat of violence continued in the Fenian raids and such things as the 'fifty-four-forty-or-fight' crisis. They then tried economic penetration, in which they were brilliantly successful. Why go to the trouble of annexing a country that is so easy to exploit without taking any responsibility for it? A society valued mainly for its beaver pelts, its softwood forests, and the soldiers it can supply for other countries' wars, is unlikely to develop any cultural phenomena beyond a problem of identity, a general state of wondering why it exists.

Part two of this history begins with the close of the Second World War. Up to 1945 immigration from countries other that the United Kingdom had been largely rural-based. But now an urbanized immigration started pouring into the larger cities: half a dozen large ethnic goups appeared in Toronto, which up till then was mainly a WASP reservation. French Canada went through a secularizing 'quiet revolution' that deprived the Catholic Church of most of its political influence, and gave Quebec a new sense of status. The indigenous people showed a strong prejudice against extinction or assimilation, and began to develop a new professional class, including lawyers, to examine such questions as whether building a golf course across land previously guaranteed to them was really in the spirit of that agreement. Meanwhile Canada had ceased to be a British colony and had become effectively an American one, which made at least more geographical sense in a post-naval world. In the sixties many American students opposed to the Vietnam draft discovered that Canada was not merely an insulation of ice against the Soviet Union but was an actual country that could be lived in.

All these developments created a cultural imbalance that exploded in the crisis of the Meech Lake controversy in 1990 and continued in the Oka confrontation a few weeks later. I am not competent to discuss the incidental problems involved here. But I feel that directly in front of us lies a primary need for what I shall call Reconfederation, and which I think of essentially as providing a cultural skeleton for the country that fits its present conditions. Without a cultural Reconfederation there can be only continued political tinkering of the most futile kind. True, I think the best political context by far for Reconfederation is a renewed political Confederation, which means abandoning all the jockeying for power that proposes trade barriers or separate currencies. I hope that the greatest of all political forces, inertia, will manifest its majestic power here.

A political entity, in any case, is not a cultural one. French-speaking Canada is a cultural reality of the highest importance: 'Quebec' is a province like other provinces, and always will be: the more separatist its policies, the more inevitably provincial their characteristics. Such pedantic fatuities as outlawing English signs on the outsides of buildings are typical of the way that the political mind works when dealing with a cultural problem. A distinct society can be only a cultural unit where a language is spoken and a culture fostered by those genuinely interested in it for its own sake, and such societies are the only possible architects of a reconfederated Canada. Quebec had been an architect of Confederation in 1867, and it has no higher destiny now than to become

leave it alone. Culture and language are an area—perhaps the only area—where privatization really does work.

The variety of ethnical mix in the bigger Canadian cities brought the buzzword 'multiculturalism' into the foreground, and a variety of problems with it. An Anglo-French bilingualism seems more problematic in a city where, as in Toronto, the Italian-speaking population is eight to ten times greater than the French one. Behind this lies the contemporary geographical situation of Canada, which is no longer at the ends of the earth but in the centre of all the great powers, the United States on the south, the Soviet Union on the north, Japan and eventually China on the west, and the European common market on the east. Two of these, the Soviet Union and Europe, are in the process of becoming primarily cultural federations. Like Switzerland in nineteenth-century Europe, Canada must now preserve its identity by having many identities.

May I revert for a moment to my conception of three aspects of culture, as a life-style, as a shared heritage, and as the pursuit of scholarship, the sciences, and the creative arts. There is hardly a distinctive Canadian cultural life-style, which has been largely identical with that of northern United States for a long time. This in turn has been part of the general homogenizing of life-styles everywhere. In Canada we say, or have said, that we are being Americanized; but America itself has become Americanized in the same way, and the original contrasts in, say, Philadelphia, St Louis and Atlanta have long since been largely obliterated.

The process here is that of the growing uniformity of technology, in which Americans have naturally had a leading role. We cannot take off in a jet plane and expect a radically different way of life in the place where the plane lands. Uniformity of standards and measurements is of course essential in all technological or mechanical areas: in other aspects of human life we seek a unity of coalescence of various things. Unity, which always possesses a quality of uniqueness, is the opposite of uniformity, where there is only likeness or similarity.

As for culture in the sense of a shared heritage, this is an outgrowth of a provincial stage where there is a sense of only one community. As the provincial grows into the genuinely cultural, the conflicts of the past become the positive elements of a common experience. *Je me souviens* is an ambiguous motto: everything depends on what one is expected to remember. If it means preserving the continuity of a cultural tradition within a larger context, it is a basic principle of human dignity; if it means brooding on suppressed resentments in the past, it is quixotic nonsense. In contrast to the United States and France, which began with revolution and the deductive approach to unity that a revolution inculcates, Canada has had a history of compromise and *ad hoc* agreements, with a fairly constant attempt, whatever the lapses, to preserve the rights of both sides. At any rate, Canada seems to impress non-Canadians as a moderate and reasonable country, potentially as happy a country to live in as the world affords. It is a peculiarly poignant irony that Canada should reach such a point when its political leadership seems to have been attacked by an epidemic of Alzheimer's disease.

The twentieth century has been mainly a period of war and tyranny: these are evil things, and there is always something unreal about evil, not for the victims, unfortunately, but in the sense of disappearing from history with no structure left behind. Nothing has improved in this century except science and scholarship, which have improved because they have no boundaries. If they do have boundaries, in other words if they are politically controlled, they soon become sinister and dangerous. And just as only science and scholarship have improved, so nothing has remained stable except the arts, including the arts of language. These do have boundaries: poetry and fiction particularly are usually limited to a very specific locale. But they are infinitely porous boundaries, open to influences from anywhere in the world. The prominence of Zola, Erasmus, Disraeli and Mill in Canadian humanist scholarship may have started accidentally through the presence of qualified scholars here, but they represent a Canadian presence in world culture, and are part of the only contribution we can make to the world that the world is likely to have much permanent respect for.

Sometimes the influence is from the same country. There are many poets and novelists in Canada of white ethnical origin who think of themselves as cultural descendants of indigenous people and helping to carry on their traditions. It is sometimes said that, for example, whites should not write about blacks or Gentiles about

Jews, but that is only froth on the surface of controversy. The more vigorous the literature, the more it thrives on cross-pollenization. One thinks of Yeats and his dependence on a Celtic and Irish mythological tradition of which he knew next to nothing at first hand. A different type of cross-pollenization occurs when a Canadian writer has a Japanese or Caribbean or Czech or Sri Lankan background.

A few weeks ago I was in Yugoslavia, travelling by train from Zagreb in Croatia to Ljubljana in Slovenia. The journey was about as far as from Toronto to Kingston, but when I got off the train I was in a different country which spoke a quite different language. For seventy years this tiny land-locked community had been a rather down-graded part of Yugoslavia, and for centuries before that an even more down-graded part of the Austrian empire. And why was I in Ljubljana? Because the university there had decided to open a school of Canadian studies. I thought to myself that this is typical of what a culture is: it is the indestructible core of a human society, so far as it is a human society and not a mere aggregate of atoms in a human mass. Such a culture can resist century after century of invasion, conquest, infiltration and neglect; yet it remains open to influences and experiences from anywhere in the world, even Canada.

The institutions of culture, museums, art galleries, and above all universities, reflect this boundary-without-walls aspect of culture in their combination of local and world-wide interests. Cultural institutions are educational as well, because what I have been calling culture is the social manifestation of the educational system. It is not only the present audience, but a rapidly increasing number of concerned Canadians, who realize that Canadian educational standards are far below what they ought to be. This question has been discussed endlessly: I have only one point to make here about it.

A very central and important aspect of education, and probably the part that stays with us longest, is what comes, not from what we are taught or read, but from what we learn from one another. The more homogeneous and provincial the community, the more of what we learn in this way is simply the repeated prejudices of our friends, backed up by similar repetitions in the news media. Canada has now become cosmopolitan to a degree that would have been incomprehensible fifty years ago. If Toronto is a world-class city, it is not because it bids for the Olympics or builds follies like the Skydome, but because of the tolerated variety of the people in its street.

Society must have loyalty, but in a democracy there are no uncritical loyalties. There must always be a tension of loyalties, not in the sense of opposed forces pulling apart, but in the sense of one feeling of belonging attached to and complemented by another, which is very often the relating of a smaller ethnical community to a larger one. It is through some such process as this that the cultural development of Canada must make its way.